Water Utility Capital Financing

AWWA MANUAL M29

First Edition

FOUNDED
1881

American Water Works Association

American Water Works Association
6666 West Quincy Ave.
Denver, CO 80235

Printed in USA

ISBN 0-89867-426-3

Contents

Acknowledgments

The AWWA Management Division Board of Trustees gratefully acknowledges the contributions made by members of the Financial Analysis Subcommittee in preparing this manual. The subcommittee's efforts aid in meeting the general need for continued improvement in financial planning by water utilities for their ongoing capital requirements.

The board also expresses appreciation to those past and present members of the committee who submitted information, drafted text, and submitted editorial comments for preparing the manuscript. The Management Division thanks the entire subcommittee for their time, expertise, and exchange of views, which has resulted in this very comprehensive financial-management manual.

Financial Analysis Subcommittee

R.D. Hardten (Chairman), Black & Veatch, Kansas City, Mo.
R.D. Ambrose, Buchart-Horn, Inc., York, Pa.
A.L. Anders, Morgan Guarantee Trust Company, New York, N.Y.
L.A. Benasso Jr., East Bay Municipal District, Oakland, Calif.
W.K. Ferry, Brown & Caldwell, Pasadena, Calif.
M.G. Hinkel, Indianapolis Water Company, Indianapolis, Ind.
J.C. Kirner, Tacoma Water Division, Tacoma, Wash.
H.G. Mülle, H.G. Mülle & Associates, Inc., Haddon Township, N.J.
P.M. Sachs, Arthur Andersen & Co., Kansas City, Mo.
L.G. Shaw, Peat, Marwick, Main & Co., Dallas, Texas
R.M. Wilson, Denver Water Department, Denver, Colo.

Management Division Liaison Representatives

E.W. Limbach, American Water Works Service Company, Charleston, W.Va.
R.L. Wubbena, Economic & Engineering Services, Inc., Olympia, Wash.

Past Subcommittee Members

K.P. Barney, Parsons Municipal Services, Inc., Pasadena, Calif.
J.J. Barr, American Water Works Service Company, Haddon Heights, N.J.
R.L. Coy, Philadelphia Water Department, Philadelphia, Pa.
Carl Goebel, Bureau of Water Works, Portland, Ore.
Fred Moriarty, Peat, Marwick, Main & Co., St. Louis, Mo.
R.W. Splete, Arthur Andersen & Co., New York, N.Y.

Other Participants

P.E. Hoback, Black & Veatch, Kansas City, Mo.
T.J. Martin, Black & Veatch, Kansas City, Mo.
J.M. Mussman, Black & Veatch, Kansas City, Mo.

Introduction

During the late 1960s and the 1970s, financial conditions of many water utilities weakened due to increases in operating costs. These increases were, in turn, due to inflation, growth-related demands, and public pressure to keep water rates low. Despite growing maintenance needs, water utilities tended to postpone maintenance in order to keep operating costs and corresponding service charges as low as possible.

In recent years, the "infrastructure crisis" in the United States has been brought to the forefront of the nation's conscience. Problems with the nation's infrastructure stem from neglect and underinvestment in the repair and replacement of public capital facilities. Deferred maintenance has resulted in higher rehabilitation costs. Even investor-owned water utilities have suffered from regulatory changes and denial of some critical rate increases, and surveys indicate that investor-owned utilities' infrastructure problems are not any different from those experienced by publicly owned utilities.

Water utilities are extremely capital intensive, requiring nearly $4.00 of gross capital investment for each $1.00 in sales revenue. For comparison, electric utilities require less than $3.00 of investment per $1.00 of revenue, while the nonregulated general business sector averages barely $0.50 of capital investment per $1.00 revenue.

AWWA strongly advocates that utility management, governing bodies, and regulatory agencies address the infrastructure crisis by realizing that customers' interests are best served through well-maintained and well-operated water systems, which assure adequate funding levels to meet utility needs. Adequate financing for infrastructure means more than limiting funding sources to federal or state grants. A variety of approaches to local financing and private ownership are also needed. Creative government assistance, where appropriate, is important; however, solutions needed for the remainder of the 1980s and 1990s may include well-structured public and private partnerships for meeting the infrastructure needs of the nation.

Thus, the subject of contemporary financing concepts is particularly relevant to the water utility industry. Many water utilities are periodically faced with increased requirements for capital funds in order to meet demands placed on their systems by rapid growth. Other utilities face rehabilitation and replacement needs. Whatever a particular water utility's capital requirements may be, knowledge of available contemporary alternatives for obtaining capital funds is a key element in developing successful financing plans.

Scope. This manual provides a comprehensive overview of traditional and innovative financing sources that should be evaluated by water utility management when determining long- and short-term financing strategies for meeting capital requirements. Only by thorough analysis of a particular water utility's long-term capital requirements and financial position will the feasibility of one or more specific financing concepts be determined.

The material presented in this manual is intended for use by both publicly owned and investor-owned water utilities. Since financing alternatives and markets may differ for these two primary types of utility ownership, unique financing alternatives for each are discussed in separate sections.

This manual covers seven general areas: strategic capital-requirements planning, strategic financial planning, financing alternatives, consideration of rating-agency requirements, special considerations for publicly owned utilities, special considerations for investor-owned utilities, and other considerations.

Proper planning of capital requirements starts with a realistic capital budget. A comprehensive budget should recognize a uniform capitalization policy; appropriate accounting records; all applicable governmental regulations; an evaluation of alternative investment opportunities; and any other considerations deemed necessary by the utility owners, attorneys, financers, and governing bodies.

Strategic financial planning involves forecasting customer demand, water sales, revenues, and operating expenditures, in order to develop an initial financing plan that reflects current and prospective utility practices.

Alternative financing methods should be analyzed and compared to the initial plan to determine any cost savings and shared benefits between the ratepayers and the utility. Alternatives should be further evaluated for their ability to meet utility objectives and rating-agency requirements.

Investor-owned systems must make special considerations for meeting financing requirements. In addition to the normal business risks of attracting capital in a manner that maintains the utility's capital structure and provides an adequate return on stockholders' investment, investor-owned utilities must balance the needs for renewals and replacements through depreciation and equity funding. Regulatory-agency decisions play an important part in the investor-owned utility's ability to meet its capital requirements. The potential effects on the utility and ratepayers of regulatory decisions regarding financing alternatives should be evaluated.

Other planning considerations consist of convincing local government, regulatory agencies, and rating agencies of the benefits of proposed plans. Well-documented strategic plans will assist in this activity. Also, since change is inevitable, sensitivity analyses of potential contingency situations should be evaluated for their impacts on utility planning. Such analyses will lead to better management decisions and problem avoidance when real contingencies occur.

A glossary at the back of this manual, which provides terms commonly used by the financial community, is a continuing step towards establishing uniformity of definitions. The glossary will be revised and/or expanded as additional AWWA financial and accounting manuals are developed.

Purpose. Information presented in this manual may have certain limitations. Water utility capital requirements continually change as do financing sources available to the utility. At any given time, the financing alternatives available to a utility will depend on (1) US tax codes and the Internal Revenue Service rules and regulations; (2) interest rates charged for various financing alternatives; (3) the utility's credit rating; and (4) decisions by governing bodies, regulatory agencies, and voters in some instances. New financing alternatives are created and old ones abandoned as market conditions change. Some financing options may become obsolete until future market changes or legislative actions make them feasible again.

This manual is not intended, nor should it be considered, as a complete text on water utility capital-financing concepts. Revisions to the tax code based on the tax acts of 1984 and 1986 are recognized.

The text should be primarily considered as a guide for determining capital requirements, strategic planning, and financing alternatives that may be applicable to a local situation. No recommendations or opinions about the relevance of alternative forms of available financing have been provided.

AWWA advocates that specific financing requirements for any particular water utility be based on sound engineering, economic, financial, and accounting principles. Often, the services of consultants and counselors experienced in such matters are required. When such advisors are employed, this document should serve as a resource that the policymakers and utility managers may draw on to guide their evaluation of the validity of any proposed financing alternative.

Chapter 1

Strategic Capital-Requirements Planning

To address the infrastructure crisis facing the water utility industry and the continuing need for plant expansion and/or replacement, water utilities will be required to systematically engage in a capital-requirements planning process. As part of the capital-requirements plan, existing facilities should be maintained in good repair through a program of scheduled maintenance. To do this, some facilities will have to be restored to full operating condition, while the utility provides for periodic expansion requirements. With each capital expenditure, utility management should ensure that the system is receiving the most value for the money spent and that total costs to utility customers are kept as low as possible.

STRATEGIC PLANNING

The strategic component of the planning process deserves special consideration. The focus of this strategic component is not so much on producing an end result as on how the planning process occurs and the considerations taken into account during the process.

While many utilities engage in capital-requirements planning, they do so in a manner that frequently concentrates on historical practices and methods of producing a single document—a capital-improvements program. Such a program is certainly an appropriate result in the capital-requirements planning process. However, there should be other products of the planning effort that indicate the effect of the capital program on the utility's service levels, financial condition, regulatory compliance, service costs, and other aspects of utility operation.

Factors Involved

Generally, there are three broad factors involved in strategic capital-requirements planning for water utilities. They include

- defining service levels and utility customers' needs,
- determining what facilities will provide the defined service levels, and
- determining the affordability of the facilities or securing the necessary resources to construct and operate them.

There are several secondary elements within each of these broader factors that, for any particular water utility, will have different importance in the planning process. While some elements are mentioned here along with their potential ramifications, management must ultimately judge the potential consequences of each as it pertains to planning utility capital requirements.

Defining service levels and customers' needs. There are several things to consider when defining service area, service levels, and customers' needs. Some of the more important items are listed below.

- Definition of service area is normally accomplished through a certificate of convenience and necessity for investor-owned utilities; publicly owned utilities generally do not have formally designated service areas. Thus, this step can be an important one from a long-range planning standpoint.
- Demand forecasting is helpful in both the short- and long-term development of capital-improvement programs; publicly owned and investor-owned utilities develop demand forecasts in essentially the same manner.
- Extension policies define the manner in which service is extended to new customers and under what conditions various payments are required of the new customer.
- Service level indicates the minimum service level provided to customers. Investor-owned utility service levels are usually more formally prescribed by state or local regulatory agencies than are those of publicly owned utilities.

The above factors can have a significant bearing on development of capital requirements. The capital planning process should intentionally incorporate consideration of these factors, as well as others that may be of consequence.

Physical facilities. After determining the service requirements, management should concentrate on the physical plant needed to provide the defined service levels. Again, there are a number of things to consider, including

- Available water supply in the short-term is essentially fixed. A major increase in demand must, therefore, be forecast well in advance to permit bringing new water supplies into existence.
- Age and condition of plant must be specifically determined with knowledge of the age and condition of the actual existing plant, as well as its capacity and capabilities. Replacement or upgrading of facilities may be needed to furnish the level of service specified earlier.
- New technology may be available to improve quality of service or to provide the same quality of service at a lower cost. If new technology is available, it may also have an effect on operations.
- Capital project administration for a major capital program may test the capacity of construction inspection and management capabilities. The program can be extended over a longer time period or outside services may be required.

Financial resources. When considering financial resources, several issues may need to be addressed. These issues, which are discussed below, concern not only the financial capability of the water utility, but also the customers' ability and willingness to pay for service provided.

- Project benefits for the customer, whether immediate or substantially deferred into the future, should warrant the cost to build the facility.
- An adequate return on investment should cover the risks involved and be sufficient to meet the acquisition financing costs.
- The potential rate effects of the capital program should be evaluated for appropriate cost recovery from existing and future customers.
- Financing alternatives should be evaluated in order to determine those alternatives that produce the lowest total cost, the lowest risk, the appropriate financing ratios, and timely project funding.

Components of the Planning Process

The issues that are to be addressed in capital-requirements planning suggest participation by personnel from nearly all functional areas of a water utility, including

- engineering and construction,
- operation and maintenance (O&M),
- finance and accounting, and
- customer service.

Planned commitment and active involvement of personnel from each of these disciplines should add immeasurably to the successful development and implementation of a capital-requirements program.

Accurate and unbiased information is also a critical ingredient to the capital-requirements planning process. For example, assessing the age and condition of existing facilities may require a continuing property records system. Additionally, knowledge of customer attitudes and satisfaction levels requires research and opinion surveys carefully designed to solicit a candid response.

Other aids to the planning process include the use of the accounting practices recommended by the National Association of Regulatory Utility Commissioners* and the Governmental Accounting Standards Board†. Such practices include the use of a uniform system of accounts, a continuing property record system, and a list of retirement units. Good capitalization policy and associated record keeping will provide management with current information for identifying and justifying capital needs on which to base capital-requirements planning.

Long- and Short-Range Goals

Strategic planning consists of developing long- and short-range goals. Although there is no definite dividing line between the two, long-range planning in this manual pertains to periods of at least two and preferably five or more years, while short-range planning pertains to annual budgeting and daily decision making that are used to implement the long-range plan. Use of long-range plans to guide short-range decisions

---

*National Association of Regulatory Utility Commissioners, P.O. Box 684, 1102 ICC Building, Constitution Ave. and 12th St. N.W., Washington, DC 20044.

†Governmental Accounting Standards Board, P.O. Box 3821, High Ridge Park, Stamford, CT 06905.

will help a utility avoid operating in a crisis-management mode when providing services.

Goals to be reached in five years or longer may be very general when timing is imprecise. The plan becomes more specific in the current years, because considerably more information is known. The test of a viable capital-requirements plan is whether utility management and policymakers systematically commit resources to implement the plan.

REVENUE REQUIREMENTS

Total utility revenue requirements consist of O&M expenditures and capital-requirements expenditures. The elements of revenue requirements are defined in the following paragraphs.

O&M

Operation expenditures include those system operating costs required during the process of providing water service. Maintenance expenditures are those costs required to maintain the system in good operating condition and include repairs or replacements of minor property components less than the size of a retirement unit.

Capital Requirements

Rehabilitation consists of expenditures, basically resulting from repair due to damage, wear, or decay to one or more retirement units, required to restore facilities to normal or optimum condition. Replacements are expenditures for property components that are the size of one or more retirement units and that take the place of other existing units, basically through substituting an equivalent item. Improvements consist of betterments or upgrades, resulting in increased value, quality, or usefulness of facilities the size of one or more retirement units. Expansion consists of expenditures to enlarge capacity of facilities or extend the system into new areas not previously served. Other expenditures consist of annual principal and interest payments on outstanding long- and short-term debt; payments to reserves required by contracts or covenants; and, for investor-owned utilities, dividend payments to stockholders required to maintain the financial integrity of the utility system.

For publicly owned utilities operating under a cash-based budgeting and fund accounting system traditionally used by governmental entities, capital requirements may be classified into two broad categories: (1) principal, interest, and reserve payments on outstanding debt, the principal of which has been used to finance major capital improvements and replacements; and (2) normal or routine replacements, extensions, and minor improvements financed from current revenue and retained earnings.

The utility basis for determining capital requirements is mandated for all investor-owned utilities and for most publicly owned systems under the jurisdiction of state regulatory agencies. Under the utility basis, capital requirements are generally defined as depreciation and return on investment.

Depreciation. For either publicly owned or investor-owned utilities, depreciation is a loss in value of facilities, not restored by current maintenance, that occurs in property due to wear, tear, decay, inadequacy, and obsolescence. The proper level of depreciation expense at any given time should be based on the costs of depreciable plant in service. The funds resulting from depreciation are available for replacements, improvements, expansion of the system, or repayment of the principal portion of outstanding debt.

Return on investment. The return component is intended to pay the annual interest costs of debt capital and to provide a fair rate of return for the total equity capital used to finance physical facilities used in providing water services. For publicly owned regulated utilities, equity is the value of facilities developed by the local government's resources, exclusive of capital contributions from others and the value of land. The rate of return for publicly owned utilities should be sufficient to ensure confidence in the financial integrity of the enterprise in order to maintain its credit rating.

Investor-owned utilities meet their capital-financing requirements through uncommitted retained earnings, depreciation funds, the sale of stock, debt issuance, or a combination of such methods. The rate of return for such utilities should not only be sufficient to maintain the utility's credit rating, but also to retain the investment of existing stockholders and to attract new capital, regardless of source.

CAPITAL BUDGETING

Within the framework of major objectives and policies established for a water utility, management must plan and control capital-expenditure activities. Planning encompasses anticipation of customer needs for water service, selection and design of proper plant facilities to meet such needs, timely purchase or construction of required plant additions, and timely replacement and retirement of plant assets. The resulting capital-expenditures plan should reflect management's understanding of strategic objectives.

The capital budget is a plan that covers all additions and retirements to existing utility plant. This budget could be segregated between major and routine capital projects. Major capital projects include proposed additions or retirements that involve relatively large outlays and are of a nonrecurring nature. Routine capital projects include proposed additions and retirements that more or less recur on an annual basis. In order to facilitate coordination of long- and short-range plans, the capital budget should be prepared for a minimum of five future years. In some cases, the capital budget may tie into a master plan of 20 years or more.

Developing the Budget

The process of developing a multiyear capital budget should integrate all aspects of planning, so that not only are the priority and timing of new facilities determined, but the impacts on all operating costs are estimated. The effect of the capital budget on manpower and material requirements serves as the basis for planning the operation and construction activities to be performed by the utility. Through this comprehensive evaluation process, the budget provides an instrument for control over capital expenditures. The multiyear capital budget should be reviewed and revised annually. The current year should be dropped, the plans for the next several years reviewed and modified as necessary, and the program extended for one additional year to encompass a new multiyear plan.

To be useful as a planning and control document, the summary of budgeted capital expenditures should be supported by individual project budgets. Normally, each individual project budget includes a project number, a description, the purpose and necessity of the project, the project's priority, the scheduled initiation and completion dates, a detailed cost estimate, the estimated incremental operating revenues and expenses associated with the project, and, if applicable, the estimated return on investment. Although it may be difficult at times to trace the actual source of funds for individual projects, it usually is desirable to identify the intended financing source.

This should help identify special financing opportunities, which may reduce the utility's total funding requirement.

Regulations

Utility management should be aware of the requirements and dictates of all regulatory agencies on the federal, state, and local levels when planning capital requirements. For investor-owned water utilities, regulatory control is usually exercised by a state regulatory agency. The authority given to these agencies is generally comprehensive. Publicly owned utilities are normally regulated by local governments. In some states, the larger publicly owned utilities are regulated by state agencies. Positive steps should be taken to ensure that the utility is in compliance with these regulatory agencies or that allowances in capital and operating budgets have been made to address deficiencies that become evident as a result of specific regulations.

Safe Drinking Water Act. In December 1974, Congress passed the Safe Drinking Water Act. The act has been amended several times, most recently in 1986. The act and its subsequent amendments, the most important legislation affecting water quality standards, require all water utilities to meet minimum national standards for the protection of public health. States have been given the primary responsibility for enforcing regulations governing health standards for drinking water established by the US Environmental Protection Agency (USEPA). This legislation has significant implications for management, especially in terms of planning for water utility facilities to meet the new water quality standards.

Since 1980, the USEPA has cited a number of water utilities for failing to meet drinking water quality standards. The identified shortcomings pertained to the lack of sufficient, full-time, and adequately trained operators; operator apathy towards federal standards; and, most significantly, insufficient funding to meet federal requirements.

Other regulatory requirements. Under public law 92-500 and public law 95-217, as amended, the USEPA also controls point discharges from water utilities into the nation's water courses. The capital requirements for meeting point-discharge permit requirements should be included in the capital budget.

Other government agencies, such as the US Department of Labor, are responsible for exercising control in the area of occupational safety through the enforcement of the Occupational Safety and Health Act (OSHA). Additionally, some water utilities must adhere to water-resource control requirements of certain state agencies.

Capital-Budgeting Techniques

Consistent with the long-term forecast of annual customer demands for water service, utility management should determine the appropriate capital projects needed to address local needs. The public-utility obligations of both investor-owned and publicly owned water utilities require that a specified level of service (quantity, quality, and service area) be provided, which directly affects the capital-investment decision. Failure to anticipate replacement or extension of particular plant facilities may result in the inability of a utility to provide a minimum level of service to its customers.

There may be a number of alternative capital projects that will meet a particular requirement. These alternative proposals for meeting plant investment requirements should be evaluated in terms of expected costs compared to expected benefits, in order to determine the best alternative from a financial viewpoint.

Investor-owned utilities have considerable experience in using capital-budgeting techniques when making plant investment decisions. Although regulated utilities are normally authorized to recover a certain rate of return on rate base, the utility is not guaranteed such a return. Regulated utilities screen investment alternatives for those that provide the highest expected rate of return (equal to or greater than the authorized rate of return) and authorize construction of such projects, to the extent possible, from their cash flow. In such analysis, the timing of the next general rate case is important. At the time of the next general rate case, the regulatory agency will probably adjust rates to provide an authorized return on the enterprise's plant investment. Because of this periodic adjustment, utilities can construct facilities that do not offer an acceptable rate of return, but will provide other public-interest benefits (i.e., improvements in water quality or, in some cases, expansion of service).

Until recently, publicly owned utilities have not generally relied on capital-budgeting techniques for investment decisions. Most capital programs result from master planning studies performed by engineering consultants or studies that have been prepared in-house. Often capital-budgeting techniques are not used, and many times political considerations outweigh financial considerations. Consequently, evaluations of alternative projects may have been somewhat limited in the past.

There are several capital-budgeting techniques that may be used to evaluate investment alternatives. Among these are return on investment, internal rate of return, and the net present-value methodology.

Return on investment. In order to use the return-on-investment method, an estimate of direct and indirect costs of the proposed investment and an estimate of the annual income resulting from the proposed investment must be made. Average annual income is the difference between the estimated change in average operating revenues resulting from the investment and the estimated change in the average operating costs from the same investment. The percentage return on investment is determined by dividing the average annual income by the investment costs.

The minimum acceptable rate of return for a capital expenditure project should be set at a level such that any return on investment greater than the required return will assist in maintaining the financial integrity of a utility, whether investor-owned or publicly owned. The return on new investment must be equal to that required to attract the financial resources of new investors and cause current investors to maintain their holdings.

The minimum acceptable or required return on new investment should be set at a level equal to or greater than the weighted average current cost of capital to the utility. Utility management should ensure that the utility is receiving the most value for the money spent, if infrastructure problems are to be properly addressed. Four important considerations in the evaluation of investment alternatives include

- the net amount of the investment;
- the returns expected from the investment;
- the expected rate of return on the investment, as determined by the previous two factors; and
- the lowest rate of return on the investment that will be acceptable to the utility.

In some cases, a project is needed to fulfill a utility public-service obligation or requirement, even though the estimated rate of return is less than the acceptable rate. Other capital projects may be considered because they reduce operating costs or expand the service area, thereby creating a potential for increased revenues. Alternative proposals for meeting the program requirements should be evaluated in terms of rate of return; however, the best alternative would generally be the one with the highest estimated rate of return.

Internal rate of return. Discounted cash-flow techniques can readily compare projects having different lives and different timing of cash flow, because discounting allows comparisons to be made at the same point in time. The internal rate-of-return method uses present-value concepts, but seeks to avoid the arbitrary choice of a rate of return in evaluating an investment proposal.

The methodology requires finding a rate of return that will make the present value of the cash proceeds expected from an investment equal to the present value of the cash outlays required by the investment. Such a rate of return can be found by trial and error. If the present value of the cash proceeds exceeds the present value of the outlays, then some higher rate of return would make them equal. The approximate rate of return that makes the two equal is referred to as the investment's yield.

The internal rate-of-return method considers only the incremental cash outlays and incremental cash proceeds associated with a particular investment proposal. Therefore, noncash expenses, such as depreciation associated with a particular investment, do not directly affect the rate of return. Depreciation expense associated with a proposed investment does indirectly influence a yield on investment of investor-owned utilities to the extent that additional depreciation charges increase cash proceeds by decreasing income taxes.

Net present value. The net present-value methodology is a direct application of present-value concepts. Computations require choosing an appropriate rate of return; computing the present value of the cash proceeds or savings expected from the investment; and computing the present value of the cash outlays required by the investment, using the chosen rate of return. The present value of the proceeds minus the present value of the outlay is the net present value of the investment.

The recommended accept or reject criterion is to accept all independent investments whose present value is greater than or equal to zero and to reject all investments whose present value is less than zero. However, care should be taken to choose the appropriate rate of return, since different rates of return may result in different rankings of alternatives. When choosing an investment alternative, the utility would select the largest net present value.

Other Considerations

In some cases, especially on mandated projects where capital-budgeting techniques indicate rejection, the return on investment or present value may be increased by obtaining greater donations or contributions in aid of construction from customers, subdivision developers, or governmental agencies. If projects must be built immediately to meet service demands but reflect an insufficient estimate of the desired rate of return, it may be necessary for the utility to increase the return by increasing water rates.

The final capital plan must be practical and include objectives that are needed and can be reasonably expected to be accomplished. Utility management must understand the capability of the utility's staff to administer the plan if the projects are to be completed on schedule. Otherwise, the cost of outside services to assist in plan implementation should be considered when formulating the capital program.

The capital budget that is easiest to finance consists of total annual expenditures that are fairly uniform or that increase at an inflation rate reflective of local construction conditions over a period of several years. In establishing the capital budget, every effort should be made to provide for uniform levels of annual capital-improvement expenditures, which are also consistent with demands for utility service. In this way, moderate and fairly uniform increases in utility rates may be achieved. Once capital projects have been identified and properly scheduled, strategic financial planning may begin.

Chapter 2

Strategic Financial Planning

With an established capital budget, utility management can develop a financing plan that will meet the cash requirements of the utility's budget. There are a number of alternative financing sources available to publicly owned and investor-owned water utilities that can be used to achieve this goal. Utility management has the responsibility to use a combination of these financing sources that will, over the long run, minimize the cost of money to the utility. With a capital budget and a financing plan developed, management is able to time its activities in money markets, in order to keep the cost of money as low as possible under the circumstances.

A single source of funds cannot be used without legal or economic limitations. Attempting to minimize the effective interest rate by accepting indenture agreements that place severe restrictions on the utility's ability to issue refinancing and new debt issues or respond to changing capital markets may not be a wise decision.

The purpose of strategic financial planning is to provide insight into a water utility's future service demands, its costs and revenue needs, and to develop a financial plan that minimizes all costs. Future service demands will depend on the mix of customer classes, changing customer-service characteristics, changes in service area, and the economics of the community. With an understanding of financial forecasting and planning techniques, a review of contemporary financing alternatives, and consideration of rating-agency requirements, management may develop a long-range strategic financial plan tailored to the utility's requirements.

FINANCIAL FORECASTING AND PLANNING PROCESS

Strategic financial planning involves comparing projections of all utility revenue sources with revenue requirements for a two- to five-year planning period. This is done in an effort to determine need for additional sources of funding and alternative financing, which will minimize effects on utility finances and charges to customers served. Projections for periods longer than five years are highly speculative. Successful financial planning requires that the effects of the capital budget on revenue and revenue requirements for the planning period be demonstrated.

One step in the planning process is to forecast revenue and revenue requirements, which consist of O&M expenditures and other capital costs expressed on a cash or utility basis (or both). Such projections are usually predicated on estimates of future customers served and water sales, representing the midground of the cyclical highs and lows of water utility service. Since projections generally represent a midpoint in utility operating cycles, most utilities provide carry-over contingency funds for periods when revenues are less than projected. Funding for such reserves may be derived from bond proceeds in accordance with indenture requirements or from retained earnings during years when actual revenues are larger than projected.

Water Sales Projections

Based on utility billing records, an estimate of the number of customer accounts by customer class should be made for a two- to five-year planning period. A review of these records should provide total annual water sales for each class. In determining an average use per customer account by class, large users should be analyzed independently, in order to minimize such customers' water-use impact on the class-average use. The selected class-average usage should represent use during a typical rainfall year, rather than either a wet or dry year. Customer account projections should be based on a multiyear trend rather than on the most recent historical year of record, the recent number of building permits issued, or a design engineer's estimate of use. Such projections should also recognize deviations from historical trends resulting from expansion of service area or loss of major customers.

For unmetered water sales, billing records provide the number of customers in the class and the estimated number of units on which water charges are based. In the absence of adequate billing units, an estimate of water usage for the class may be made from production records, knowledge of meter sales, and an estimate of unaccounted-for water. Unaccounted-for water may range from 10 percent for new facilities to over 50 percent for older utilities, depending on the adequacy of historical repairs and maintenance. In other cases, master meters may be installed on water mains for sampled groups of unmetered users to provide estimates of each class usage.

For financial-planning purposes, conservative and realistic projections of customers and water sales are advisable. Optimistic growth assumptions may cause financing problems for the utility if growth does not materialize.

Revenue Projections

All sources of revenue and income should be reviewed when developing financial plans. However, sound utility financing dictates that revenue from the sale of water and closely allied services should cover the costs of providing water service. Nonoperating income, contributions in aid of construction, and other charges should be recognized. In rapid growth areas, such sources of capital funds can become major components of utility funding. However, successful implementation of the plan should not be solely contingent on receipt of such monies.

Projections of water-sales revenue should be based on the projections of customers and water sales developed concurrently for the financial plan. The number of customers served, an analysis of water use by usage blocks, and the existing schedule of charges should be used to project revenue by customer class, and in total, for each year of the planning period.

Nonoperating revenues should be evaluated for those items of a recurring nature that potentially may be available in the planning period. A realistic level should be estimated for such revenues. Recognition of infrequent sources of nonoperating revenue, such as a sale of utility property, should be minimized even though future receipts are anticipated.

O&M Projections

The National Association of Regulatory Utility Commissioners' uniform system of accounts classifies O&M expenditures by the following functional expense categories: source of supply, pumping, water treatment, transmission and distribution, customer accounts, and administrative and general. Within each category, some costs will vary more than others with the production and sale of water. Power for pumping and chemicals for water treatment are considered to vary generally with the sale of water. Personnel costs and certain material and supply costs are considered to be reasonably fixed, in that these expenditures vary more with the size of the system rather than with the variable sale of water. Changes in such fixed costs are gradual and tend to be increases that are due to the effects of inflation on costs or pay-plan decisions. Some costs, such as meter reading, meter installation, and customer-related services, may vary with the number of customers served, and are typically referred to as customer costs.

A review of historical records should indicate long-term trends and the appropriate basis for projecting a particular expense. At the same time, a determination should be made whether historical relationships will continue to exist in the future. Regardless of the basis chosen for projecting changes in expenditure levels, all projections should recognize the long-term effects of inflation on costs. However, caution should be exercised if it is assumed that short-term, or current, inflationary trends will continue for a multiyear planning period.

Finally, an adjustment in the level of O&M expenditures should be made for significant increases in costs projected by the capital budget when new facilities become operational. Expenditures should recognize changes in personnel, power, and other operating costs caused by revisions to utility plant.

If utility staff will be used during construction of facilities, some recognition for capitalizing a portion of the expenditures should be made in the plan. Publicly owned utilities typically budget all personnel, materials, and supplies in an operating budget. To the extent that budgeted expenditures are to be paid from sources other than operating revenue, such sources of capital funding should be used as an offset to budgeted operating expenditures, in order to reduce impacts on utility revenue. Care should be taken to ensure that capital-related work by utility forces is accounted for only once, in either the operating budget or capital budget.

Capital Expenditures

For publicly owned utilities, capital expenditures consist of payments for existing debt service, various reserves, and routine capital projects normally financed from annual revenue. A schedule of future annual debt service is established when the existing debt was incurred and is a matter of public record. Estimates of routine capital expenditures normally financed by revenue are developed in the capital budget.

For investor-owned utilities and regulated publicly owned utilities, capital costs consist of depreciation and return. Depreciation is based on utility plant investment, estimated service lives, and variable depreciation rates by class of property. For long-range financial planning purposes, depreciation may be estimated from existing plant in service, plus anticipated additions to utility plant, less anticipated retirements during the planning period. Return would then be the allowable rate of return applied to the utility's projected rate base. Frequently, regulated utilities are faced with actual return realized being less than the allowable return. For financial planning purposes, a conservative and realistic estimate of return should be used.

Although investor-owned utilities' capital requirements are expressed differently than those of publicly owned utilities, regulated utilities should determine revenue requirements on a cash-needs basis as a check on the adequacy of total utility revenue. In some cases, analysis on the basis of regulation reporting, tax reporting, and application of cash funds should be prepared to provide management with full information for financial decisions.

Other Considerations

Additional financing requirements. Publicly owned and investor-owned utilities are generally faced with additional financing requirements. For example, publicly owned utilities frequently must pay to the local governmental entity a franchise fee, payments in lieu of taxes, and/or internal-governmental fund transfers. Investor-owned utilities must consider income taxes, property taxes, franchise fees, and dividend policies.

Record keeping. Good record-keeping practices are essential to the financial planning process. Such records would include customer billing data, continuing property records, cost accounting systems, and construction work-in-progress accounts. Accounting and budgeting policies and procedures should be compatible with the financial planning process.

INITIAL FINANCIAL PLAN

Once projections of the various components of revenue and revenue requirements have been completed, a cash-flow forecast and analysis can be made to compare annual revenue and revenue requirements for the planning period. The cash-flow analysis should include an initial beginning balance, which excludes all funds committed for current liabilities and construction work in progress. Each year, uncommitted carry-over funds should be shown as available to meet future capital requirements.

As an initial plan, the flow-of-funds analysis should recognize the historical means by which the utility has financed all revenue requirements and has met major capital program expenditure needs. The plan should demonstrate that annual revenues from the sale of water are adequate to meet the cash requirements of O&M expenditures, payments for existing and proposed debt requirements, and routine capital expenditures financed from revenue.

After the initial financial plan has been developed, a review of financing alternatives is in order. The initial plan provides a basis for comparing effects of financing alternatives on revenue and revenue requirements, as well as on utility customers served.

Effects on the Ratepayer

In determining what effects a potential financing plan has on the utility ratepayer, careful consideration should be given to the methodology used. Assumptions that an across-the-board, percentage-rate increase will result in a corresponding percentage revenue or billing increase may be reasonable under certain conditions. If a recent cost-of-service study has been conducted and the percentage increase is reasonably small, reflecting minimal changes in the mix of capital program expenditures and consistent customer-service requirements, then an across-the-board increase can likely be made, and the increased revenue from customer bills will reflect across-the-board changes.

If there is a significant change in any of the requirements stated above, then the effects on the utility ratepayer are best determined through an updated cost-of-service study. Significant changes may affect customer classes differently, in that costs to be recovered and revenues received from some classes may increase faster than others. Allocation methodologies, which depend on plant investment or utility rate base, may indicate a significant shift in allocated costs between classes, if there are significant plant additions in one functional area. Furthermore, effects on ratepayers may depend on class service requirements, which may have changed considerably since the most recent cost-of-service study had been conducted. A change in the rate form used to recover class costs will also have an effect on the ratepayers' bills.

Typical bills are a common means of determining effects on the ratepayer. Such bills could show a variety of meter sizes and water use by customer class, in order to provide an indication on how increases will impact the class as a whole. Another method is to use the median-use bill of the class; by definition, half of the bills have usage greater than and half of the bills have usage less than the amount on the median-use bill.

Chapter 3

Financing Alternatives

Once an initial financing plan has been developed, alternative financing techniques should be reviewed to determine which techniques meet utility goals and also result in more effective and less costly ways to finance capital requirements. For the alternatives that are considered, separate cash-flow analyses should be developed and compared to the initial plan and to other alternatives in order to determine the best course to follow. In some cases, assistance from a consultant well versed in financial matters may be necessary. Alternative financing of capital requirements may include annual system revenue, debt, equity, contributions, grants, leases, and privatization.

SYSTEM REVENUES

Internally generated funds, or system revenues, can be used to finance plant improvements. "Pay-as-you-go" financing is practiced to some extent by most water utilities. The funds generated annually by rates and charges that are not used for O&M expenses or for debt payment can be used for replacements or new construction. In some utilities, annual revenues for such purposes may be limited to replacement of vehicles or other equipment. However, more utilities are increasing the funding from this source in order to reduce their debt burden or reliance on other alternative financing during periods when the cost of borrowing is high.

The amount of funds generated from system revenues can vary greatly. In a system that uses revenue bonds, funds generated in excess of actual debt-service requirements for coverage purposes are available for financing improvements. To enhance bond ratings, coverage is sometimes increased above minimum levels, making additional funds available. Such funds can also be accumulated for financing major projects.

An investment strategy may involve increasing revenue for several years prior to project construction in order to generate partial project funding and to smooth rate increases over time. A decision should be made as to whether customers will be more willing to pay a small increase over a longer period of time, with a possible stepped increase when final project financing is determined; a large single-rate increase at initiation of construction for project financing; or large increases at the time of placing the new facilities in service. With sound long-term planning, including investment of temporarily available cash during construction and accurate bond issue sizing, the effect on customer rates can be minimized, and the use of excess funds may be properly planned.

To determine whether potential financing plans will meet utility goals and objectives, and receive public acceptance, analyses of the effects on each utility's ratepayers should be conducted. Although direct effects may be easily determined and readily apparent, indirect effects are not always obvious. Use of revenue above a reasonable level may increase rates to current users, although the benefits may accrue more to future users.

LONG-TERM DEBT FINANCING

For large and infrequent major capital projects, utilities normally use long-term debt to spread the cost of the project over a number of years. This is done to keep annual revenue requirements low and to ensure that future users of the system help pay for the project. However, utilities should not jeopardize their financial structure by using too much debt, thereby, reducing their credit rating and incurring abnormally high interest costs. Revenue-financed minor extensions and replacements help to keep the financial structure intact. An optimum mix of revenue and debt financing of capital requirements can be obtained that will keep rates low to current customers and recognize that future users who will benefit from the system should share in such costs.

With the issuance of long-term debt, contractual obligations to conduct utility business in a specified manner are incurred. However, such obligations could be too restrictive in the financial flexibility afforded the utility. Consequently, bond covenants for existing or proposed debt should be carefully reviewed by management before agreeing to a specific financial plan.

Conventional long-term debt financing consists of general-obligation bonds and revenue bonds. However, in recent years, local government issuers have faced high and frequently volatile interest rates, unfavorable economic conditions, and decreased federal assistance. During this same period, demand for improved public services has increased, stricter environmental and safety standards have escalated the costs of constructing water facilities, and the need for massive infrastructure repairs and improvements has become more evident.

In response to this situation, a complex array of innovative long-term debt, credit enhancements, and short-term financing techniques have been used or developed. In general, these innovations seek to improve the security and marketability of the bonds for resale, provide market-price protection, shorten maturities and thus lower interest costs, obtain higher credit ratings, or enable renegotiation of the interest rate. Generally, official statements of government issuers must include an opinion of bond counsel confirming the tax-exempt status of the debt instrument. The 1984 and 1986 tax acts substantially limit the ability of agencies to issue debt that is fully tax exempt by restricting the use of bond proceeds.

General-Obligation Bonds

General-obligation bonds are debt instruments backed by the full faith and credit of the issuing unit of government. The bonds are secured by an unconditional pledge of the issuing government to levy unlimited taxes to retire the bonds. A government's general-obligation pledge is usually regarded by investors and the rating agencies as the strongest form of bond security, and thus generally represents the lowest cost of financing available to local governments.

Certain general-obligation bonds are secured not only by the issuer's general taxing powers but also from additional revenue sources, such as specific fees, grants, special charges, or net revenues of a water system. These bonds are sometimes referred to as combination bonds or "double-barreled" bonds, because of the dual security provided by revenue and tax sources. In many cases, the debt service of such bonds is, in fact, totally paid by enterprise revenues without any tax support.

General-obligation bonds are the most traditional, well-known form of tax-exempt borrowing. This type of bond financing can benefit the issuer in a variety of ways. First, due to their strong security features, the interest rates of general-obligation bonds are generally the lowest available and can result in considerable interest savings. Similarly, this unconditional pledge of tax revenue, as well as investor familiarity with this traditional standardized form of financing, make general-obligation bonds very marketable. Costs of issuance are generally lower than those associated with revenue-bond financing, not only because it costs less to market a bond with wide market acceptance, but also because the documentation associated with general-obligation issuance is less complex than that required for revenue-bond financing. Because general-obligation-bond financing does not require the restrictive covenants, special reserves, and higher debt-service coverage associated with revenue bonds, current revenues are not unnecessarily restricted, or pledged, and can be used for other purposes.

While the issuance of general-obligation bonds has many advantages, there are also certain drawbacks to this form of financing. One of the most significant drawbacks is that new taxes to support new general-obligation debt must generally be authorized by the electorate. In addition to obtaining voter approval for new bonds, issuance of general-obligation debt may also be limited by local-government debt ceilings and interest-rate ceilings.

Revenue Bonds

Revenue bonds are used to finance local-government or public-enterprise projects that generate revenue and are expected to be self-sustaining. Principal and interest on the bonds are secured by and payable exclusively from revenues received from system operations or from the project being financed. No taxes are levied or pledged as a backup. Revenue-bond debt-service payments usually come from charges paid by the users of the water system.

Revenue bonds are issued to provide initial financing for facilities that can pay for themselves over the investment's useful life. The market acceptance of revenue bonds is highly dependent on the service or project to be financed and the issuer. Such bonds present a greater risk for the investor than do general-obligation bonds, since repayment of the debt depends on timely completion of the project, an adequate rate or charge structure, and sound fiscal management of the enterprise. Revenue bonds generally command higher interest rates than do general-obligation bonds because of greater risk perceptions.

To provide investors and the rating agencies with financial assurances that enhance marketability, most revenue-bond indentures contain the following security elements:

- a *revenue pledge* that all revenues derived will be used first to pay all O&M costs and then all debt service due, reserve-fund requirements, and any costs associated with system repair or replacement;
- a *rate covenant* by which the issuer agrees to enact rates sufficient to meet costs and that indicates the number of times current net revenues must cover debt service and other costs;

- an *additional bonds test* in which both a historical and a projected revenue test may be used to avoid the dilution of coverage below established levels on outstanding debt; and
- a *reserve fund* specifying an amount, usually expressed in terms of average or maximum debt service due in any future year, required to be held as a cash reserve for annual debt-service payment to the benefit of the bondholders.

The revenue-bond form of financing offers important benefits to the issuer. Unlike most tax-supported debt, revenue-bond issuance does not usually require voter approval. A voter's right to petition for a referendum is, however, generally available. Revenue bonds also avoid possible and unnecessary dilution of the government's full faith and credit pledge, since such bonds are not included in the issuer's debt limit.

There are also a number of disadvantages to the use of revenue-bond financing. In most instances, revenue bonds carry higher interest rates than do general-obligation bonds. This is a result of the more limited security that revenue issues typically offer to investors and, quite possibly, the more limited market among investors due to certain institutional restrictions regarding underwriting criteria. Higher interest rates and marketing difficulties are particularly apparent with regard to enterprises without established earnings potential or a history of financial operations.

Documents associated with revenue bonds usually incorporate requirements for special reserve funds and debt-service coverage ratios, as well as limitations regarding the amount of future debt that can be issued.

The indenture requirements of existing debt have a significant impact on the choice of financing alternatives. First of all, rates must be established at a sufficient level to meet all bond-covenant requirements. Coverage, although not usually a cash requirement, is a test of revenue adequacy. If the cost of capital projects financed with revenues is sufficiently large, the revenue generated to meet these requirements will be sufficient to demonstrate that the utility is meeting its coverage requirements. If a utility is not spending enough revenue on planned capital projects, then the coverage provision would govern, resulting in the need for more revenue than identified cash requirements. In the latter situation, coverage-generated revenue that is not used for capital projects provides a built-in current-revenue reserve for meeting system emergencies.

The existence of restrictive financing provisions, associated with indentures of outstanding revenue bonds, often make it difficult to issue additional bonds and may trigger the refinancing or refunding of outstanding debt. Refunding, if appropriate, should be made part of the established financial plan.

Finally, initiating a revenue-bond program is more complex and generally requires more time than general-obligation borrowing. Revenue bonds usually have higher legal, engineering, and trustee fees. Projects to be financed need a demonstration of engineering and financial feasibility. A revenue-bond issue's added cost has important implications for an issuer. In some instances, benefits of revenue-bond financing may not be worth the cost. A variety of factors, such as total debt, issue size, rating, and bond proceeds, should be considered in making the choice between revenue and general-obligation bonds.

Bond-Structure Variations

To increase revenue and general marketability, investment houses use a variety of bond structures to address specific market conditions (Table 3-1). For example, during periods of high interest rates new structures were developed that resulted in better marketing. Historically, such structuring has included tender-option bonds (put bonds), floating-rate bonds, floating-rate monthly demand bonds, original-issue discount bonds, zero-coupon bonds, compound-coupon bonds, stepped-coupon bonds, and bonds with warrants attached. Such variations may ultimately place more of the investment risk on the issuer in order that the bonds may be placed, thus subjecting the issuer to substantial market and interest-rate risk.

Tender-option bonds (put bonds). Tender-option bonds, or put bonds, are long-term bonds that provide the investor with the option of tendering the obligation back to the issuer, generally at par, well in advance of the stated maturity. This put option creates a potentially shorter-term obligation. A put option can attract long-term investors while taking advantage of short-term interest rates. During a period of steep yield curves, a put option enables an issuer to sell bonds at a rate substantially below prevailing long-term rates, since the issue has characteristics of a short-term obligation.

Put options traditionally follow one of two structures. A *window put* can be exercised once during a certain period, such as on a particular day or month in the future. An *anniversary put* enables an investor to tender the bond back to the issuer periodically, usually once every year. Tendering the bond once a year is customary, beginning three to five years after the date of original issue.

To protect the issuer from the risk that a majority of the bonds might be tendered at one time and to assure investors that there will be sufficient funds available to redeem bonds if the put is exercised, a bank letter of credit (LOC) from a major financial institution must generally be provided.

The most significant advantage of tender-option bonds is the interest savings that can be achieved. The interest savings can be substantial, but will vary with market conditions, the credit rating of the issuer, and particular put-option features. However, the letter-of-credit fee, any insurance premiums, and the cost of funds potentially borrowed against the letter of credit can offset potential savings.

Floating-rate bonds. Floating-rate, or variable-rate, bonds are securities whose interest rate is pegged to one or more market indices or interest rates. Although the rates on some issues are tied to the prime rate or a composite index of long-term rates, most are sold on the basis of the treasury market, with certain adjustments. The bonds are typically subject to a specified floor and ceiling on the rates. This protects issuers from paying rates considerably higher than anticipated and, at the same time, guarantees the investors a certain minimum yield in low-interest-rate markets.

The frequency at which rates are adjusted varies. A monthly or even semiannual adjustment is common for long-term bonds, while rates may be adjusted weekly on short-term instruments. Floating-rate bonds are extremely popular investments in a volatile bond market where rates fluctuate rapidly, since they preserve the market value of the bond.

One primary outcome of floating-rate debt is that the issuer assumes the interest-rate risk. Therefore, investors are willing to accept initial rates considerably lower than those of comparable fixed-rate securities. This can result in considerable interest-rate savings for the issuer. While lowered interest costs may be attractive to issuers, there are some disadvantages associated with floating-rate debt. Issuers face great uncertainty in planning future debt-service requirements and establishing revenue needs when bond interest costs can vary greatly. Floating-rate debt is also more expensive to administer and requires greater administrative expertise than fixed-rate debt. Finally, floating-rate bonds are generally attractive to investors only during periods when interest rates are expected to rise. Marketing of floating-rate

Table 3-1 Summary of Bond-Structure Variations

Features	Tender-Option Bond	Floating-Rate Bond	Floating-Rate-Monthly Demand Bond	Original-Issue Discount Bond	Zero-Coupon Bond	Compound-Coupon Bond	Stepped-Coupon Bond	Bonds With Warrants
Market-Rate Expectations								
Rising		X				X	X	
Volatile	X		X					
Declining				X	X			X
Long-Term Investors	X	X	X	X	X	X	X	X
Short-Term Features	X	X	X					X
Interest Rates								
Initially low	X	X	X	X		X	X	X
Variable by index		X	X					
No current interest					X			
Convertible to fixed			X					
Bonds of common rates							X	
Yield to Maturity								
Near market rates			X				X	
Lower than market rates	X	X		X	X	X		X
Deferred Principal or Interest			X	X	X	X	X	X
Tax Considerations				X	X			
Issuer Assumes Risks								
Unfavorable market		X	X	X	X	X	X	X
Call option penalties				X		X	X	
Tender options	X		X					
Separate market vehicle								X
Required Protection								
Letter of credit	X		X					
Sinking fund			X		X	X		
Proceeds Received								
At par	X	X	X			X	X	X
Below par				X	X			
Administrative Costs								
Higher		X	X					X
Lower					X	X		

bond issues is, consequently, limited to those periods when higher interest rates are predicted, and cannot necessarily be relied on as a financing method at other times.

Floating-rate monthly demand bonds. The concept of long-term floating-rate monthly demand bonds (lower floaters) was developed in response to chaotic conditions in the traditional long-term tax-exempt market. In this market, investors were reluctant to commit funds to long-term fixed-rate bonds due to significant losses incurred from the previous purchases of such securities. In a market where interest rates for long-term bonds remain high, the majority of issuers will still prefer to finance debt for as long a term as possible.

Long-term floating-rate monthly demand bonds are similar to floating-rate demand notes. The bonds are sold with a stated maturity of up to 30 years (or longer if permitted by state law) and with no scheduled principal amortization prior to maturity. The bonds are subject to optional redemption at par by the borrower at any monthly interest-payment date. A bank or insurance-company letter of credit must accompany the bonds. A sinking fund is generally established to provide for redemption of the bonds at maturity.

Interest on the bonds is paid monthly and is determined based on an evaluation of short-term issues of tax-exempt securities with the highest credit rating, such as commercial paper and project notes. The issuer, through the appointment of an indexing agent, determines the interest rate on the bonds by setting forth a formula for the indexing agent to follow in determining such a rate. On a onetime basis, the issuer may alter the original terms of the bonds to convert from a floating to a fixed interest rate. The fixed rate is derived from a long-term index composed of comparably rated issues with similar maturities.

The bonds are usually issued in denominations of $100,000. They are placed primarily with tax-exempt money-market funds or other large institutional buyers.

The most obvious advantage to this form of financing for the issuer is the very attractive initial rate, as compared to fixed rates. Other benefits and risks are similar to those discussed for floating-rate bonds. Floating-rate monthly demand bonds are not appropriate for all municipal issuers or public enterprises, and not every municipal issuer can obtain the letter of credit that is requisite to the transaction.

Original-issue discount bonds. Original-issue discount (OID) bonds are long-term bonds that have an interest rate substantially lower than prevailing market rates. They are sold at a discount, for an amount considerably less than the face value of the bond. The difference between the original cost of the bond and its stated value at maturity combined with the amount earned as interest payments over the life of the bond is used to calculate an OID bond's yield to maturity.

This financing method relies on Internal Revenue Service (IRS) rulings that the capital gains resulting from the difference between the purchase price and the value of the bond at maturity are exempt from taxation. Because not all bonds originally offered at a discount are exempt from capital gains tax, the opinion of bond counsel must confirm the tax-exempt status. The 1986 tax act has substantially reduced capital-gains tax considerations, which probably will result in the cessation of the structure's use in the foreseeable future.

The OID bonds have two primary advantages for the issuer: lower interest costs and, generally, a lower overall yield to maturity. There are a number of reasons why investors are willing to accept a lower yield and lower interest income from OID bonds. In states where the face value of a discounted bond can be used to meet pledging requirements, the same dollar amount can buy considerably more face value of OID bonds than of conventional bonds. Similarly, individual investors can purchase a large par amount of bonds at a relatively low cost. Since the reinvestment risk is primarily born by the issuer, OID bonds are particularly attractive during periods when interest rates are expected to decline and only lower-yielding reinvestment options are anticipated. They are also advantageous during periods of active tax swapping when there is considerable demand for discount bonds.

A disadvantage of OIDs for an issuer is that the issuer must sell a greater par amount of bonds in order to realize the same amount of bond proceeds. This could present problems if the issuer's legal debt authorization is limited. Another consideration for an issuer is that early redemption of the OID bonds is expensive. Exercising call provisions at premium or even par can raise the yield on the bonds considerably.

Zero-coupon bonds. Zero-coupon bonds are long-term bonds that pay no interest prior to maturity. They are originally sold at a substantial discount from par. Holders of zero-coupon bonds receive no current interest income from the bonds. Investor income is paid as the difference between initial cost and redemption value. Such bonds are also known as capital-appreciation or deep-discount bonds.

Because issuers of zero-coupon bonds assume the full reinvestment risk, investors are willing to accept a lower yield to maturity than with conventional bonds. Issuers also incur fewer administrative expenses, since they are not making semiannual interest payments.

The low initial price of zero-coupon bonds, compared to their value at maturity, appeals to individual investors for whom a $5000 bond would be prohibitively expensive. Zero-coupon bonds are often purchased to provide money for future educational or retirement needs. They are attractive investments for investors who wish to maximize long-term gain with a minimum of reinvestment risk. A disadvantage of zero-coupon bonds for investors is their price volatility prior to maturity during periods of interest-rate swings. Also, issuers must carefully structure appropriate sinking-fund provisions to assure that requisite funds are available at maturity to meet balloon payments due at that time.

Although zero-coupon bonds can provide considerable interest-rate savings for an issuer, they can present some difficulties. Some states prohibit excessive discounting of bonds. In other instances, state or local debt limitations or maximum-debt authorizations may inhibit the sale of zero-coupon bonds. The concept of issuing bonds with a par value many times greater than bond proceeds may be difficult to sell to the public. Also, the 1986 tax act has substantially reduced capital-gains tax considerations, which will probably result in a cessation of this bond structure's use in the foreseeable future. The issuance of compound-coupon bonds may be preferred.

Compound-coupon bonds. Compound-coupon bonds, also referred to as deferred compound-interest coupon bonds, are long-term debt securities sold at par value. Semiannual interest accrues to investors at a compounded rate, but is not paid until maturity. This form of financing is similar to zero-coupon bonds in that it enables the issuer to defer interest payments until maturity, but it avoids problems that zero-coupon bonds pose for some issuers, such as an inability to sell bonds below par or an inadequate par amount of debt authorization. Because investors have no reinvestment risk, they are willing to accept a lower rate of interest on the bonds.

These issues can be structured either with level debt service to the issuer, incorporating higher principal payments in the earlier years that decline as maturity increases, or with a balloon payment at the end that is funded through sinking fund payments.

The advantages of compound-coupon bonds to the issuer include somewhat lower interest costs and reduced administrative expenses. It can enable an issuer to defer all debt service on the bonds until maturity, which can be particularly helpful for start-up enterprises. However, since relatively few of these issues have been marketed, the secondary market acceptance is not tested, and interest savings at the time of issuance have not been substantial. Additionally, the cost of redeeming compound-coupon bonds prior to maturity is high.

Stepped-coupon bonds. Stepped-coupon bonds are bonds designed to provide a market yield over the life of a bond issue, but to defer considerable interest cost to more distant years. In this innovative financing, all outstanding bonds, regardless of maturity, bear the same rate of interest every year. This common rate increases by steps in later years.

Stepped coupons are an inflation-oriented approach, borrowing heavily into the future. They can provide considerable interest savings in an inflationary environment, but could prove very expensive to the issuer should the rate of inflation be substantially reduced.

Because of the weighting of interest in the future years, stepped-coupon bonds are prime candidates for refunding. In order to reduce this probability and increase marketability, call premiums may run as high as 30 percent, greatly increasing the costs of the issuer's early redemption options. Stepped-coupon issues are not appropriate investments for those unwilling to hold the bonds until maturity.

Bonds with warrants attached. A warrant attached to a bond entitles the bondholder to purchase future bonds at the same price and interest rate as the original issue. An investor, betting on a decline in interest rates during the period of time the warrant is valid, accepts a lower rate of interest on the original bond issue. This lowers the interest costs to issuers and broadens the market for municipal debt to include speculative purchasers.

Warrants may also be detached from the bonds and sold separately, thus creating an additional market for the securities. Issuers must be prepared to issue additional bonds at rates higher than prevailing market rates, should interest rates decline sharply enough to prompt the use of the warrants. The probability that the warrants will be exercised depends on future interest-rate trends. Issuers can limit their risk exposure by issuing bonds during a period when stable or rising interest rates are predicted or by limiting the period of time during which the warrants can be used.

Municipal Credit Enhancement

Well-publicized municipal-bond defaults, volatile bond markets, and governmental fiscal problems have increased investor concern over the quality of long-term municipal securities. In response to concerns about the credit worthiness of municipal issuers, various external credit supports have increasingly been used to enhance the security of bonds that often might not otherwise be sold. Two of the most significant credit-enhancement vehicles available to issuers are municipal-bond insurance and bank letters of credit.

Municipal-bond insurance. As a credit enhancement, bond insurance enables low-rated issuers to obtain an investment-grade rating and, consequently, to trade at lower interest rates than their own credit rating would normally allow. For the cost of a one-time premium, the municipal insurer guarantees the entire debt service on the bonds. With this guarantee, the bond issue will be assigned a triple-A bond rating by Standard & Poor's Corporation (S&P). Moody's Investors Service, Inc. (Moody's), however, does not take the insurance into account, and they rate an insured issue the same as any other noninsured series of bonds by the same issuer.

There are some disadvantages and risks associated with use of municipal-bond insurance. The up-front insurance payment is deducted from bond proceeds, thereby, reducing the amount of funds available for construction projects. Even with an investment-grade rating, insured bonds seldom perform as well in the market as comparably rated uninsured bonds, in part, due to the disparity in rating-agency opinions on insurance. Higher costs to customers accrue if offsetting lower interest rates are not significantly different than the anticipated interest rates without insurance.

Bond insurance may not be available to all issuers. In order to spread their risk, insurers may have limited underwriting capacity in certain geographic areas or with regard to particular types of bond issues. Insurers also frequently impose restrictions on bond issues they underwrite, including requiring reserve funds, high coverage requirements, or rate covenants.

Letters of credit. The use of letters of credit (LOCs) by water-bond issuers, as well as other municipal-bond issuers, has expanded even more rapidly than private bond insurance. Both Moody's and S&P will raise the rating of issues backed by LOCs to the rating of the bank issuing the LOC.

In general, LOCs are provided by major banks with the highest investment-grade ratings, although regional banks have also issued them for local bond issues, sometimes with a "cover" LOC from a major bank. If this rating is higher than the rating an issue would have received without the credit support, there will probably be interest savings resulting from the LOC support.

An LOC on a bond issue generally represents an unconditional pledge of the bank's credit to meet debt-service payments promptly, in the event an issuer defaults on the bonds. An irrevocable LOC is similar to municipal-bond insurance in that the credit risk on a bond issue is shifted from the investor to a third party at the issuer's expense. Since few banks choose to extend their exposure beyond 5 to 10 years, most issues supported by LOCs have relatively short maturities or are structured to provide for retirement of the debt prior to expiration of the LOC. Bonds issued for shorter periods have higher annual principal payments than might otherwise be the case, resulting in a greater financial effect on utility financing.

The cost of securing an LOC can add measurably to the ongoing expenses of a bond issue. The fee charged is generally payable on an annual basis and represents a fixed percentage of the amount of bond funds secured by the LOC. In addition, utility administrative costs may increase because of requirements to file regular financial reports with the bank issuing the LOC. Despite these drawbacks, LOC support can produce considerable interest savings for an issuer. Also, LOCs are a requisite component of such financing techniques as tender-option bonds, floating-rate monthly-demand notes and bonds, and tax-exempt commercial paper.

Interim Financing

Interim or short-term project financing typically includes short-term borrowing instruments with maturities of less than one year, including bond-, tax-, grant-, or revenue-anticipation notes; tax-exempt commercial paper; and floating-rate monthly demand notes. The security for interim financing ranges from anticipated tax revenue to LOCs. Short-term notes or borrowing instruments are generally purchased by investors unwilling to commit to long-term funds. Interim financing has been common with investor-owned utilities but, historically, has seen limited use by municipal utilities.

Interim financing is often used to take advantage of lower short-term interest rates at the start of a project and to pay for design, property right-of-way acquisition, equipment purchases, and initial project construction. Interim financing can also be used to avoid long-term financing commitments in high-interest-rate markets. The issuers intend to refinance the short-term obligations with long-term debt once market conditions improve. This use of interim financing permits project construction to begin on schedule, even in high-interest-rate markets, and can reduce total interest costs for the project during construction. Interim financing can also eliminate the need or desire to refund long-term debt issued during high-interest-rate periods.

Short-term borrowing can be advantageous to an issuer, since it may provide lower total project costs through lower interest costs during construction. However, interim financing is not intended as a long-term solution to utility financing. Although utilities may "roll" short-term notes until construction is completed, long-term debt must eventually be issued.

Disadvantages of interim financing do exist. Multiple-transaction costs for a number of rolled notes may offset the advantages of more precise borrowing. Furthermore, short-term borrowing typically assumes that long-term interest rates are expected to fall; however, a utility may be faced with issuing bonds during unfavorable market conditions. The threat of becoming overburdened with short-term debt is also a potential disadvantage to the use of interim financing. Significant amounts of short-term borrowing by an issuer can raise credit concerns and, consequently, increase the interest costs of long-term borrowing.

Bond-, tax-, grant-, and revenue-anticipation notes. Notes are promises by a municipal issuer to repay an amount of money from a specific revenue source, such as a future bond issue (bond-anticipation note, or BAN), anticipated revenues (revenue-anticipated note, or RAN), taxes (tax-anticipated note, or TAN), or grants (grant-anticipated note, or GAN).

The major advantage of issuing BANs, RANs, TANs, or GANs, in lieu of long-term bonds, is the lower interest rate. At risk, however, is the issuer's ability to enter the long-term bond market at rates below current interest-rate levels when the notes mature. If rates do not decline measurably, future financing costs may increase. Also, if legislation permits, the temptation to rollover the outstanding notes with another short-term issue may overburden the municipality with short-term debt.

Tax-exempt commercial paper. Tax-exempt commercial paper (TECP) is a short-term promissory note with an average maturity of 30 to 45 days. The notes, which have a maximum maturity of 270 days, are intended to be refinanced (rolled-over) continuously for periods that may exceed one year. The TECP differs from other interim financing in that it must be rated by the national rating agencies and supported by a bank LOC or a similar credit facility, which enhances the cash liquidity of the issuer, protecting the investor in the event a new issue cannot be sold when a maturing issue becomes due.

The use of TECP by municipal issuers has increased measurably in recent years. The primary advantage for an issuer is the extremely low interest born by TECP. Because of the very short maturities, superior credit quality, and the ready liquidity of TECP, it is a prime investment instrument for the tax-exempt money-market funds. Due to the strong demand for short-term tax-exempt securities by funds and individual investors, the interest rates on TECP are the lowest of all tax-exempt instruments, typically trading as much as one full percentage point below comparable one-year financings.

There are, however, a number of disadvantages to TECP financing. The initial start-up and operating costs of such a program are typically greater than those of alternative short-term borrowing methods. These costs include the cost of a bank LOC, bond counsel fees, and transaction costs associated with administering the program. Consequently, $25 million is the generally accepted minimum issue size. Once TECP has been issued, the recurring refunding and sale process, which gives it the characteristics of a continuous-securities offering, requires daily staff commitment. Issuers also assume all the risks of short-term borrowing when issuing TECP. Depending on market conditions, the maturing issues may not be able to be refinanced with new commercial paper. If the LOC is drawn on, the new loan will probably carry a taxable interest rate.

Floating-rate monthly demand notes. Floating-rate monthly demand notes can be used to provide long-term financing, but they are also used to meet short-term financing needs or provide project construction funding.

The notes are sold with no scheduled principal amortization prior to maturity and are subject to optional redemption at par by the borrower at any monthly interest payment date. On the first day of each month or at any time on specified prior notice, the holder of any note has the option to demand that such note be remarketed and receive par value, plus accrued interest. The remarketing agent (designated at issuance) remarkets any such note, using these proceeds to pay the prior holder the principal amount of the note.

Interest on the notes is paid on the first day of each month, and the interest rate on the notes is adjusted monthly. To enhance marketability, the notes have the benefit of an irrevocable LOC or a revolving credit facility issued by a large bank or insurance company.

Floating-rate monthly demand notes or bonds are usually issued in $100,000 denominations and are placed primarily with tax-exempt money-market funds or other large institutional buyers. Since the notes are extremely liquid, secure, and tax-exempt, they generally bear a lower interest rate than longer-term issues.

The most obvious advantage to this form of financing for the issuer is the lower initial rate, as compared to fixed rates. There are, however, other advantages, such as low issuance costs, lower bond size as compared with conventional issues, no call premium, and the opportunity to earn interest on unexpended funds during the construction period. The most serious drawback of floating-rate financing is the risk of rapidly increasing costs during periods of interest-rate rises. This form of financing is not appropriate for all municipal issuers or public enterprises, since not every municipal issuer can obtain the LOC that is requisite to the transaction.

EQUITY FINANCING

In a publicly owned utility, equity is the net worth of the system, equivalent to total assets less liabilities. At a point in time, for example, the close of a fiscal year, retained earnings consist of annually generated revenue and other income that may or may not be committed to pay for ongoing capital projects. A utility that uses uncommitted equity to finance some capital expenditures will generally be able to borrow at a lower rate than a utility that relies exclusively on debt financing. Also, new debt financing generally increases revenue requirements to be met by utility charges.

For an investor-owned utility, common equity consists of common capital stock, paid-in capital, and retained earnings. When the cost of debt is high or in the interest of balancing the capital structure, such utilities tend to rely more on the use of stock issuance and internally generated funds for construction.

If time is critical, equity financing expedites the start of construction, because the money is already on hand. In addition, the utility could take advantage of periodic down cycles in the construction market. Use of equity financing reduces the need for additional debt financing. On the other hand, equity accumulated by a utility results from revenues generated from current customers. A selected project should be carefully chosen so that current customers are benefitted more than future users.

CONTRIBUTIONS

Customer contributions of money and property can serve an important role in water utility financing. Historically, customer contributions have been related primarily to customer connections and distribution system facilities. Customers have been required to purchase their meters and pay for the installation of taps and services. Developers have been required to provide distribution mains, fire hydrants, and customer connections for new subdivisions as contributions in aid of construction. While these contributions relieve a water utility of some of its capital needs, they do not generally provide financing for supply, treatment, and transmission facilities.

Some utilities require developers to make customer advances for construction of subdivision facilities. The utility then reimburses the developers during a specified period, as new customers connect to the system. Any funds remaining at the end of the period are retained by the utility as contributions in aid of construction.

After 1986, investor-owned utilities were required to treat contributions as taxable income. Such contributions include money and the value of property received.

Contributions for publicly owned utilities may also include previous or current intergovernmental fund transfers, covering a portion of capital requirements for specific facilities. The local government's sources of funding, such as general-obligation-bond proceeds or property- and sales-tax revenue, would not affect the utility's revenue level, since repayment is not usually intended.

Contributed funds permit the utility to ensure that new users share in the risk of utility service. Contributions may be used to expand service into new areas or reduce effects of rehabilitating or upgrading facilities. In either case, the utility may keep costs to be recovered by current revenues lower than might otherwise occur. Contributions may help to postpone or reduce in size future revenue increases. They may also be used to pay for reserve capacity that existing customers may have paid the carrying costs on for a number of years. Where contributed funding is used, current customers do not subsidize growth or rehabilitation to the same extent as where all customers pay total utility costs on an average-cost basis.

Contributions, as part of capital-finance planning, are difficult to recognize because they can be an inconsistent source of funds. Receipt of contributions usually depends on growth cycles and the demand for utility service. For those capital projects in which a utility shares construction costs with others, the utility may have particular difficulty planning the timing of such project expenditures.

GRANTS

Development of public water supplies has traditionally been a local responsibility. Unlike the wastewater industry, there has not been a large federally funded grants program tailored for the water industry.

However, there are grants available from various federal and state agencies for rural or economically depressed areas. The Farmers Home Administration (FmHA) provides grants and loans for rural water and sewer systems and communities with populations less than 25,000. Economically depressed areas have received help through programs administered by the Economic Development Administration (EDA), the Department of Housing and Urban Development (HUD), and the Appalachian Regional Commission (ARC). Some states, such as Wyoming, Colorado, New Jersey, Oklahoma, Pennsylvania, and North Carolina, provide grants or loans in some limited instances.

Use of grant funds can generally help utilities keep total costs of new construction low to current users. Total grant funding of capital projects does not necessarily place an increased requirement on utility revenues. With partial grant funding, in which the local utility's share is a small percentage, there may sometimes be a tendency for local governments to oversize system or facility capacity, because the utility's money goes considerably further. Such oversized facilities may not work efficiently, which may result in higher O&M expenditures. As the utilities share of cost responsibility increases with declining grant funds, and if compliance with the grantors requirements are mandatory, the financing of capital cost could become a burden on existing customers.

Most grant funding requires increased reporting and strict compliance with grant provisions, which may necessitate that the utility incur unforeseen expenditures at a future date or outright repayment of the original grant itself. Overly strict grant requirements may decrease the utility's flexibility for financing utility-capital requirements.

With reduced federal spending, a result of current budget-cutting policies, little, if any, grant monies appear to be available in the near future. This will be true even though federally mandated potable water quality standards may burden local funding sources. The obligation to provide alternative and adequate sources of funding to meet federal requirements has been placed on local utilities.

LEASING

Leasing is an alternative form of equipment or facility financing that may be applicable for some water utilities. Leasing is complex, involving tax benefits to the lessor and tax implications to the lessee, and is subject to the interpretations of the IRS. Utility managers should be aware of the need for proper legal assistance in undertaking leasing and the numerous tax rulings that must be complied with when structuring a lease. Tax laws are constantly changing, and a knowledge of applicable laws must be considered when a lease is to be entered into.

The tax acts passed in 1984 and 1986 substantially reduced the benefit of tax-oriented leasing. Most equipment leased to a utility is not subject to the investment tax credit nor the rapid depreciation for tax purposes of the accelerated cost recovery system (ACRS). Exceptions are made for certain classes of equipment. In addition, the 1986 tax act repealed the investment tax credit deduction. This lessens the attractiveness of direct leases and substantially reduces the benefits of leveraged leases, both of which are described in detail below.

Leases may still be attractive for municipal utilities as a means of acquiring the use of needed equipment and facilities, where debt limitations restrict direct purchase and ownership. Normally, a utility can acquire or bring facilities on line quicker and with less red tape through lease arrangements with private parties. Because there normally are fewer delays due to regulation with private development, there is potential for lower project costs. Most leases are written such that the utility would have an option to buy at the end of the contract period. Maintenance during this time would be the utility's responsibility. Consequently, the value of facilities at the end of the lease depends on how well they are maintained during the agreement.

Major sources of lease financing include large banks, equipment manufacturers, real estate development firms, and major leasing companies. Most firms will provide preliminary lease-rate quotes, which may be used to compare lease costs against ownership costs. Because lease rates and terms may vary, obtaining several preliminary quotes for detailed analysis is advisable.

Direct Lease

Under a direct lease, the lessee (utility) first makes decisions concerning needs. Any special features desired, capacity, terms of guarantees (when needed), construction, and services are specified by the lessee at the outset. The lessee also negotiates the price and term of the lease, the rental or service charge, and other necessary and optional considerations with the lessor. The parties then enter into a lease agreement.

After the lease is signed, the lessor purchases the equipment or constructs the facility exactly as specified in the lease agreement. When the equipment or completed facility is delivered, the lessee formally accepts it to make sure all specifications are met. The lessor pays the purchase or construction cost, and the lease goes into effect. Rentals paid by the lessee are income to the lessor. Costs for O&M typically are the responsibility of the lessee and may not be deducted from rentals.

At the end of the lease term, the lessee usually has the option to renew the lease, purchase the equipment or facility, or terminate the agreement and return the equipment or facility to the lessor. The options available to the lessee at the end of the lease are very significant in that the dimensions of such options determine the nature of the lease for tax purposes and the classification of the lease for financial accounting purposes.

Leveraged Lease

A leveraged lease is similar to a nonleveraged, or direct, lease, but it is more complex in terms of size, number of parties, documentation, legal involvement, and the unique advantages to all parties.

The leveraged lease transaction involves three key parties: the owner/lessor (a corporation, partnership, or taxpayer(s)), the user/lessee (the utility), and the lender. The lessor owns the facility for tax purposes and becomes the owner by providing only a percentage (20 to 40 percent) of the required amount to be invested. However, the lessor is entitled to federal tax benefits based on 100 percent of the cost of the equipment or facility.

The primary tax benefits of this kind of lease include income-tax deductions for depreciation of the property and income-tax deductions for the interest paid on loans used to finance the lessor's acquisition of the equipment or facility. The lessor also receives cash income from the rentals paid by the utility under the leaseback arrangement. The lessee is responsible for O&M of the facility. The lender, in exchange for putting at risk the remaining 60 to 80 percent of the cost of the item, holds a security interest in 100 percent of the leased equipment, or facility, and the revenues therefrom.

The most obvious benefit of a leveraged lease is low cost. A lessor can offer lower cost by passing on a portion of the tax savings. A disadvantage of a leveraged lease is the complexity and initial cost in arranging such financing. Transaction costs of 8 to 9 percent may be involved.

Certificates of Participation

An alternative lease–purchase arrangement is offered by certificates of participation, which rest ownership liabilities with the lessor and give the lessee (the local government) control over all certificate features. The lessor issues certificates to third parties to finance equipment or property acquisitions and incurs the liability. The lessee controls the features of the certificates through the lessor's articles of incorporation, lease and agreement with the lessor, an ordinance passed by the local government, and/or the mortgage and trust indenture.

Restrictions placed on the lessor, concerning use of property and disposition of lease payments, establish security for the certificate holder and the basis for tax-exempt interest payments from the local government.

The lessor is entitled to receive proceeds from several sources. The most important income source is the base rental payments under the lease. The lessor is also entitled to payments representing the annual business costs for paying agent and registrar fees. If property loss exceeding a specified value occurs, the lessor would receive insurance proceeds to retire an equivalent amount of certificates. If the property is liquidated, proceeds would first be used to pay certificate holders in proportion to outstanding principal amounts, with any remainder being paid to the lessee.

Other advantages exist for the lessee. Financed property is aggregated by expected useful life, so the lease would provide for the release of certain equipment prior to the final payment for the whole class. Also, an established purchase-option price is equivalent to a call privilege for bonds and normally starts halfway through the lease period.

However, disadvantages do exist. The removal of equipment from the lease prior to its expiration is viewed by rating agencies, investors, and insurance companies as dilution of the transaction's security. The purchase option may be exercised earlier in the option period, if lessee-generated revenue is used, rather than later in the option period, if proceeds are derived from borrowing or subsequent lease–purchase financing. Advance refunding is permitted, but interest-rate protection is provided to investors who are taking a risk that rates will not increase substantially, causing the market value of the certificates to decrease.

PRIVATIZATION

Privatization refers to private-sector ownership and or operation of facilities and services used by government entities in performing their public function. The concept of privatization is as old as investor-owned public utilities, which are perhaps the ultimate form of privatization. The term *privatization* came into vogue after the federal income tax amendments of 1981. That tax act focused attention on private-sector tax benefits that could be shared with the public sector, thereby, lowering the cost of facilities for the public sector. Subsequent tax acts limited the tax-related savings, and recently enacted tax reform measures all but eliminate them.

However, privatization will continue to provide advantages in certain applications, just as it did prior to the 1981 tax act. Privatization may be advantageous for projects requiring expenditures beyond the financing capabilities of a government entity, areas subject to sudden technological change, and rapid expansion of the need for services and facilities. In some cases, privatization permits the utility to take advantage of operational expertise that the utility is unable to attract because of local payroll or working provisions.

As applied to the construction of new water system facilities, privatization arrangements cover the financing, constructing, owning, and operating of a facility that provides a service to a publicly owned utility and serve as a basis for obtaining revenue to compensate the investor. Public- and private-sector organizations customarily prefer to engage their own legal, financial, and bond counsel to structure such a privatization package. Like leasing, privatization may be undertaken between an investor and a public agency or between an investor and a private enterprise.

The basic privatization agreement may contain a provision for the local government or private enterprise to exercise a purchase option at the fair market value when the option is exercised. As with a leasing agreement, users (water-service customers, for example) pay fees to the public or private agency, based on rates set by the agency, to cover its administrative costs and its contractual periodic payments to the privatization investor–owner.

A fundamental necessity in establishing the basic privatization undertaking is the independence of the agreement and the investor from rate- and profit-setting jurisdiction of state public-utility regulatory agencies. In the state where a facility is to be located, the statutes delineating the jurisdiction of that state's utility regulatory authority, in large part, determine the tax status of privatization. If a "public utility" or some other defined entity over which the regulatory authority has jurisdiction includes a firm operating a water treatment plant serving a retail water utility, the firm's property may be deemed to be public utility property.

Another statutory problem for privatization may arise out of a state's limitation on long-term contractual commitments by a municipality. Such a restriction may be found in some states' rules for public procurement of services. Thus, a desirable feature in a privatization undertaking with a local government is that there be no statutory constraint against the government's entrance into the customary long-term agreement that makes the undertaking advantageous to the investor. Without such a feature, the investor may be subject to additional risk.

In addition to potential cost savings and added financing capabilities, privatization may expedite construction if local government's procurement constraints can be bypassed. Privatization is even more complex than leasing and, therefore, must be carefully structured to ensure satisfactory construction and operation of the planned facilities for the duration of the agreement.

Chapter **4**

Rating-Agency Requirements

Rating agencies periodically review and update credit ratings for publicly owned utilities with outstanding general-obligation-bond or revenue-bond issues. The credit risk of new bond issues is also normally evaluated by rating agencies. Therefore, the financial plans that are developed by a utility should incorporate credit-agency review requirements that cover existing bond covenants and other considerations, to the extent practical.

EXISTING BOND COVENANTS

Rating agencies are particularly concerned about the degree to which a utility follows through on implementing bond covenants designed to protect bondholder's interests. For revenue-bond issues and for certain general-obligation-bond issues backed with a pledge of utility revenues, rating agencies are interested in the nature of revenues pledged for the security of the bonds, the priority of revenue uses, rate covenants, and coverage achieved through financial planning.

Covenant on Revenues

Existing bond resolutions and ordinances generally specify a pledge and lien of particular revenues to meet the utility's financial requirements of O&M expense, debt service, reserves, and other capital-related expenditures. Total revenue for bond-covenant purposes is sometimes defined to include operating revenue; nonoperating revenue, such as interest earned or rentals from nonutility facilities; and contributions, such as charges for system development. Operating revenues may be defined as income from the sale of water or the provision of closely allied services, such as cost recovery for physically connecting customers to the system.

The use of operating revenue to meet bond covenants is more realistic than the use of all revenue sources, because operating revenue essentially shows the capabilities of existing customer levels and charges for service to meet outstanding obligations. The use of total revenues, which include interest earnings and contributed capital, provides more risk, because there are no assurances that utilities will continue to annually receive significant interest earnings on invested idle funds or that growth will continue as experienced or estimated.

Operating revenues as well as total revenues should be properly evaluated. Total revenues may be used if appropriate consideration is given to reserves to meet occasional swings in interest income or growth charges used to pay certain obligations. Existing bond covenants and regulatory requirements may also have a bearing on the evaluation.

Net revenue may be determined by using either the total or operating revenue definitions less O&M expense. For revenue bonds, net revenue is a financial term, not an accounting term. In financial terms, O&M expense must be continuously met if the enterprise is to be financially successful. Such expenditures benefit both the existing customers and bondholders. The calculation of net revenue should be carefully defined in bond covenants to avoid ambiguity.

Use of Revenue

Bond covenants normally specify the order in which utility revenues are to be used. Bond "funds" are actually restricted accounts, with monies deposited therein to be used in a specified manner. Normally, utility revenues are first spent on O&M expenditures. Then, monies are usually paid into a debt-service fund, consisting of an interest account and a principal account. Next, reserves are established to provide for emergency debt-payment protection or unforeseen operating requirements. Such reserves should be fully funded in accordance with bond covenants and replenished in the event monies are used.

In some cases, reserves for repairs and replacements are established to protect the bondholders investment, by providing funds to keep the system in good operational repair. Covenants may establish the reserves for emergency use only, with infrequent use and replenishment, or as a flow-through account with monies routinely expended and replenished.

A financing plan should show that the utility's cash needs are being met over a planned time frame, such that sufficient working cash is available within the planning period. As an example, an enterprise's governing board may establish a policy to consider annual, biennial, or triennial rate increases. If rates are to be left unchanged for two or more years, the financial plan should show that sufficient reserves are built up during the first half of the rate period to finance an expected deficit in the latter half of the rate period. Total revenue and available funds should be sufficient to meet each year's cash requirements during the rate period.

Rate Covenant

In revenue-bond ordinances or resolutions, local governments pledge to fix and collect rates and charges at a level sufficient to provide revenue to meet all bond-covenant requirements. Not only will utility revenue meet annual cash obligations, but a specified percentage of revenue will normally be generated that is greater than a particular debt-service level. Usually the debt service specified is the largest in the current or any future year.

Rating agencies are particularly interested in the frequency and magnitude of rate revisions for a utility. The frequency shows local governments' willingness to provide sufficient funds to meet outstanding obligations; the magnitude is an indication of the periodic level of rate change. Small, frequent changes will lessen the rate shock on individual customers and are preferred by the rating agencies as an indication of good management.

Coverage

Annual coverage tests of earnings vary considerably between utilities. Rating agencies do not look for current fads in coverage requirements. The agencies do look to see that, for the specific utility, the enterprise has determined the level of coverage necessary and prudent for the local situation.

Coverage is based on the utility's financial ability to support debt service for each lien ranking involved. For rating agencies, it is meaningless to show coverage by lien ranking. When the prospects of a junior lien bond are uncertain, senior lien bonds are not considered as high quality, no matter what coverage is demonstrated.

Bond coverage is normally desired to ensure the availability of money to pay annual debt service and to provide for other necessary expenses of the utility. If coverage is based on net revenue, the monies available after the payment of debt service provide revenue for financing a portion or all of routine capital requirements and major capital expenditures from revenue. Coverage monies are also available to assist established reserves in meeting system emergencies.

For new bond issuance, most existing bond covenants require an earnings test, which is typically based on actual historical earnings. However, some bond covenants provide flexibility by adjusting historical earnings to recognize recently implemented rates or by providing that an independent consultant may attest to the future earnings capabilities of the utility. If a publicly owned utility is seeking municipal bond insurance, coverage is usually specified at a minimum of 125 percent of maximum or average annual debt service. Whatever the requirements, credit analysts expect to review pro forma net revenue figures supported by a report documenting assumptions, procedures, and calculations used in the financial planning process.

OTHER RATING CONSIDERATIONS

Even with the best financial planning, there are certain factors evaluated by rating agencies over which a utility's control may vary. Such areas include utility management, economics of local government and the community, accounting systems, budgeting procedures, and use of bond proceeds. The Government Finance Officers Association of United States and Canada* publishes a comprehensive document titled *Disclosure Guidelines for Offerings of Securities by State and Local Governments,* that discusses matters important to the rating process.

Management of the Utility

During each credit review, rating agencies evaluate the skills and experience of top utility managers and the governing board. Not only are resumés reviewed, but on-the-job performance is evaluated through financial and operating statistical analyses. The governing body may be a local government of elected representatives or an appointed board. The degree of board independence from local governments and stated powers is carefully evaluated. The governing body's record of fiscal stewardship over utility operations is reviewed, including a review of the physical condition of the facilities.

---

*Government Finance Officers Association of United States and Canada, 180 N. Michigan Ave., Suite 800, Chicago, IL 60601.

Local Government and Community

A primary concern of rating agencies is the wealth and income, economic stability, and growth potential of the local community. Demographic and economic indicators are carefully screened. The economic health of the community has a direct effect on the financial situation of local governments. In addition, certain local governments are restricted by spending limitations imposed through state constitutional amendments. Restrictions may result in downgraded ratings by the agencies. Local government's capability of managing finances and the willingness to provide rate relief for local utilities are evaluated.

Accounting System

Rating agencies check that a uniform accounting system is established in accordance with industry standards. Double-entry bookkeeping and accrual accounting should be used. Sufficient control should be in place to ensure adequate reporting of utility activities. In addition, annual financial reports should be attested to by independent auditors.

Budgeting

Annual budgets are used by rating agencies to determine the degree of utility planning and the direction in which utilities are progressing. Budgets disclose past and proposed fiscal policy. Budgets also indicate controls established to improve utility performance, as a measure of management capabilities.

Use of Bond Proceeds

In credit-risk review, rating agencies evaluate how bond proceeds are proposed to be used. Expenditures for replacements, system upgrades, and increased dependability are considered to provide less asset-earning power than expenditures for expansion to serve new customers. Capabilities designed into the system to meet seasonal peak requirements are considered to provide less asset-earning power than those facilities designed to provide base load requirements. The reasoning is that investment in system capacity designed to meet peak rates of use by existing customers does not normally result in the same proportional increase in annual water sales revenue as do facilities designed for customer growth and increases in total water sold. This is somewhat dependent on the rate structure used by a specific utility. Basically such analysis emphasizes that growth-oriented communities are better credit risks than nongrowing or declining communities.

Financial Plan

Rating agencies find summary information derived from a utility's financial plan, such as a two to five year cash-flow forecast, particularly useful in evaluating performance. By reviewing data from the utility's financial plan, the rating agencies gain an insight into the appropriateness of the utility's forecasting assumptions and the sophistication of its management.

Chapter 5

Additional Alternatives for Publicly Owned Utilities

Two additional financing alternatives available specifically for publicly owned utilities include special-assessment districts and system-development charges. Once these and other financing alternatives have been reviewed and incorporated into the financial plans of a publicly owned utility, the effects of alternatives on the utility and customers served may be evaluated.

SPECIAL ASSESSMENTS

Normally, local governments will establish special-assessment districts for capital projects associated with network improvements. The purpose of the districts is to ensure that those benefitting from the projects pay all costs associated with them. This, in turn, keeps the costs of providing water service to current customers and those not served within the special-benefit area as low as possible.

Establishing the assessment district before construction begins is universal. The general theory of levying special assessments within defined areas to finance improvements serving such areas requires appraising the benefits accruing from improvements to a given parcel of land. Benefits, in this context, include the provision and value of service rendered. Appraising the benefits to a given parcel requires determination of whether services are provided and of the cost responsibility for the value of services provided.

Basis for Assessment

The basis for assessment, which generally achieves the goal of benefit determination and cost responsibility determination, depends on the type of project to be financed. The two most common measures for determining special assessments are front footage and area, such as square footage or acreage. Ad valorem basis is used but primarily as a limitation or adjustment in connection with the front or square footage methods.

A special-assessment district is required to be formed at the request of a majority of the property owners. How the "majority" is determined varies. The basis may be acres of land, owners of land, and/or resident owners of land. In many local governments, the public vote within the district can be forced; however, this is rarely done. The most common way to allow public comment is the use of public hearings early in the review process.

After a project has been constructed, most local governments do not permit layered or second-benefit districts to be formed within the first district for the same type of improvement. However, there are exceptions. A new district could be formed, but the assessment basis would normally have to be changed. A change in the assessment method would be allowed if an error in the basis of assessment has been discovered or an error in the amount of the improvement was noted. However, boundaries of such improvement districts could not be changed. Where additional benefits can be shown to be needed or actually do exist, and additional financing for those benefits has been arranged, a second assessment can be levied on the original assessment district if related to an improvement already constructed. However, such an assessment is made only for the funds needed for the additional facilities that are to be constructed.

Problems

Two important pitfalls to avoid when using special-assessment districts are the improper sizing of the district and the extensive oversizing of capital projects. When sizing special-assessment districts, it is important to include all property that receives benefit or potential benefit from the proposed facilities. A clear description of the district boundaries is imperative. Capital projects should not be sized for providing service too far into the future. Frequently, oversizing of capital projects places an undue burden on the existing property owners. Planned stepped expansion of new service 5 to 10 years into the future will help minimize public opposition to proposed facilities.

The revenue received from special-assessment districts is used to pay the debt service on special-assessment bonds issued for financing the capital projects. Interest rates on these bonds are generally higher than general-obligation tax-supported bonds or revenue bonds. This reflects the smaller base supporting revenue generation and the fact that special-assessment bonds are of interest to a smaller investment market than are general-obligation or revenue bonds. In addition, there are increased requirements and costs associated with administering each district.

SYSTEM-DEVELOPMENT CHARGES

Many local government water utilities have instituted or are planning to institute fees designed to generate contributions from new customers for financing major-facilities construction. These fees may be called system-development charges, impact fees, facilities investment fees, system-capacity charges, system buy-in charges, front-end charges, or a number of other names. The charges may be based on the incremental or marginal cost of providing water service, the average per-customer cost of the utility's facilities or of equity in facilities, or some other measure. The charges may also simply reflect an estimate of the value of the service to be provided.

System-development charges are more commonly found in high-growth areas, where considerable sentiment exists to have "growth pay its own way." The magnitude of the charges range from several hundred to several thousand dollars for residential connections. Funds from such charges are used for a variety of purposes, commonly for financing capital improvements and paying debt service.

Advantages and Disadvantages

System-development charges are a viable source of financing for publicly owned water utilities. The charges can be supported by analysis and have withstood legal challenge. During peak periods of the building cycle, system-development charges can generate considerable revenue. However, since charges are tied to growth cycles, the flow of funds will fluctuate with local and national economic conditions. Funding instability is a primary disadvantage of relying on such charges to meet costs associated with current or annual revenue requirements.

Increased management efforts are required when using system-development charges in order to avoid erratic financing requirements and water-rate-charge increases. Another perceived disadvantage is the potential to discourage growth. However, utilities with some of the highest system-development charges appear to be in the nation's highest growth areas, suggesting that such charges do not discourage growth. System-development charges allow growth to pay for itself better than most other financing systems.

Chapter 6

Special Considerations for Investor-Owned Utilities

Capital-financing considerations for investor-owned utilities differ from those of publicly owned utilities. The presence of marketable common equity, a generally more rigid regulatory environment, and the economic impact of income and property taxes all must be considered by investor-owned utilities when choosing a capital-finance plan. It should be noted that regulation of investor-owned utilities is normally standardized for similar service utilities within a jurisdiction, and this may place some restraints on the extent to which a company may use each alternative source of capital.

Current tax laws, which make certain financing alternatives attractive to publicly owned utilities, do not always have a similar advantage for investor-owned utilities. However, investor-owned utilities have the opportunity of attracting equity capital in a competitive marketplace; this opportunity is not available to publicly owned utilities.

GENERATION OF FUNDS FOR CONSTRUCTION

Traditional sources of funds for water plant additions, replacements, and expansion include

- retained earnings from operations that are reinvested in plant;
- customers' advances and contributions in aid of construction or property used for construction;
- debt in the form of long- or short-term bonds, notes, and other instruments; and
- equity funds supplied by investors, in the form of common or preferred stock.

Internal Sources of Capital

Depreciation accruals/retained earnings. Actual sources of funds for a specific project will depend on a variety of financial circumstances and timing. Funds for routine replacements and renewals, to the extent possible, are normally generated internally from depreciation accruals and retained earnings. These expenditures do not usually constitute substantial investments and, therefore, do not warrant external funding. Renewals and replacements typically include replacement of service lines, meters, and hydrants, and the purchase of minor equipment items, office furniture, and tools. Funds for renewals and replacements are discussed in more detail later in this chapter.

External Sources of Capital

Typically, major capital projects cannot be funded from funds generated in normal annual operations because of the magnitude of the expenditures associated with these projects. For major construction projects, external sources of capital must be secured. Utility management must recognize the need to formulate a capital-funding program that will ensure that water plant facilities will be adequate to meet the utility's obligation of providing safe and reliable water service on an ongoing basis.

Contributions in aid of construction/customers' advances. In certain cases, external funding for construction is obtained by direct contributions from those customers who will benefit from the construction. For example, main extensions to housing developments are typically paid by developers and may be accounted for in the form of a contribution in aid of construction or as customers' advances for construction.

Contributions in aid of construction represent any cash, services, or property that is permanently contributed by customers for construction purposes. Customers' advances for construction also represent contributions from customers. However, the utility and customer enter into an agreement whereby the utility will refund part or all of the construction cost over a specified time period. Any balance remaining at the end of the agreement period is annually transferred to the contribution-in-aid-of-construction account, to evidence its permanency.

While it is possible for an investor-owned utility to benefit from some revenue growth without additional capital investment, this is normally not the case. In cases where contributions lead to revenue growth, existing customers benefit from the averaging of cost recovery for supply and treatment over a larger revenue base. However, for rate-making purposes, contributed plant is normally excluded from the rate base. In such cases, the utility cannot recover an annual return on those dollars. Annual depreciation on the contributed plant is permitted in several jurisdictions. Over time, the utility will be confronted with replacing the contributed plant and will need to increase water rates to reflect the need for additional capital requirements in long-term financial planning.

Debt–equity financing. Construction of major new facilities, such as impounding reservoirs, treatment plants, transmission mains, distribution reservoirs, and rehabilitation of distribution mains, generally requires external funding through debt or investor-supplied capital. Questions do arise regarding this external funding—Does the way in which a project is financed impact the utility; and if so, what is the optimal capital structure (debt–equity ratio)?

Selection of debt or equity financing is a complex process, and detailed analysis is beyond the scope of this discussion. The debt–equity mix for a regulated utility may be strongly influenced by regulatory perceptions of the optimum capital structure but, in most cases, is regarded as the prerogative of management, so long as the structure is prudent. Utilities will tend to secure additional debt–equity financing on the basis of maintaining or improving credit, continuing a reasonable capital-attracting ability, and optimizing return considerations.

ATTRACTING CAPITAL

For investor-owned water utilities, a primary objective of management is to attract and retain capital investment, while minimizing the effect on rates. Principal sources of capital are bonded indebtedness (short-term and long-term), preferred stock, and common stock. Contributions in aid of construction and advances for construction, as sources of capital for investor-owned utilities, are customarily limited in use to growth development and other potentially high-risk circumstances, and will have a relatively minor impact on the overall capital structure until the utility pays required refunds.

In order to attract capital investment at minimum cost, a balance in the use of the various alternative sources of capital and the rate structure necessary to generate required revenues must be maintained. In addition, a water utility must first provide safe, reliable service to its customers, maintain a respected public image, and evidence sound financial management. Further, the utility's properties must be efficiently operated and maintained, a factor that also contributes greatly to customer satisfaction and reliability of service.

Balanced Use of Debt and Equity

The most economical overall cost of capital usually results from a balanced use of debt and equity. According to financial statistics published by AWWA and the National Association of Water Companies,* the average capitalization is as follows:

	Maximum %	Normal %
Bonded indebtedness	60	52
Preferred stock	12	6
Common stock (including retained earnings)	50	42

These industry norms for capitalization vary from time to time as the economy and individual utility needs dictate. Circumstances peculiar to each utility may necessitate a capitalization structure somewhat different from the ranges stated. The relative security of each major capital source dictates different earning levels, with bonded indebtedness generally requiring the lowest return, followed in order by preferred stock and common stock.

Bonded indebtedness. Bonded indebtedness is normally secured by a mortgage of the utility's property. It has the highest lien, or call, on the utility's assets; that is, interest payments on bonded indebtedness customarily must be paid before dividends can be paid on preferred and common stock. In case of liquidation, bonded-indebtedness principal is repaid prior to refunding of stock. Therefore, from an investor's viewpoint, bonded indebtedness is the most secure and least risky form

*National Association of Water Companies, 1725 K St., N.W., Suite 1212, Washington, DC 20006.

of capital investment in an investor-owned utility. Accordingly, the cost of this debt is lower than that for preferred or common stock.

Preferred stock. Preferred stock is the second least-risky investment. Its dividends and, in case of liquidation, its principal are payable before such payments are made to holders of common stock. This hybrid between debt and equity is generally considered comparable on a risk basis to debt with a junior lien. Thus, its cost is higher to the utility than debt but not as high as common stock.

An imbalance in the debt–equity ratio used by a utility may result in overall increases in operating costs due to increased costs of capital. If, in the viewpoint of investment markets, either bonded debt or preferred stock is used excessively, the overall costs of these capital sources will increase. Furthermore, the difference in cost between them diminishes with each new issue.

Common stock. Heavy use of common stock equity does not tend to have as great an effect on its costs, or return, requirement as excessive use of bonded debt or preferred stock. Greater percentages of the higher-costing common equity does tend to increase both the protection and financial strength, as well as the overall cost, of capital. However, dilution in earnings per share with increased stock issuance may make the stock less attractive to investors.

Regulatory Lag

A major hurdle in keeping a water utility attractive to potential investors is the lag between the time that additional revenue is needed and the time that rate relief is granted by the regulatory agency. This is called regulatory lag. While state regulatory agencies have done much in recent years to accelerate consideration of rate-relief requests and to alleviate the impact of lag, a degree of lag cannot be practically avoided. Therefore, regulated utilities must maintain vigilance of their revenue needs and file for rate relief as frequently as necessary. A utility that shows itself to be progressive in maintaining adequate rates will be more successful in the capital marketplace.

To determine revenue needs, most regulatory agencies require the use of historical year expenditures that can be modified to reflect known and measurable changes. Capital markets, on the other hand, look at the future likelihood of repayment. From the perspective of innovative financing, the use of projected test years can allow the utility to be better prepared to develop a financial plan that is meaningful to both regulators and capital providers.

Interests of Investors and Consumers

The interests of investors must be balanced with the interests of consumers. Investors need to feel secure that the utility has a sound financial position and that a reasonable return is earned on their investment commensurate with the risk associated with that investment. Consumers are interested in receiving reliable service at reasonable rates. Additionally, consumers must be informed that the ability to continue to provide reliable service depends on the utility's maintenance of a sound financial position, as well as a reliable physical plant, which is necessary to attract needed capital at reasonable rates. If charges for service to customers are kept at inadequate levels, service may be obtained at the expense of future service inadequacies and/or greater levels of increases than otherwise may be needed in future charges.

A number of financial and operating ratios and indices are used by potential investors when analyzing the financial soundness of an investor-owned utility. These include calculation of rates of return, earnings coverage of interest costs and preferred stock dividends, gross and net plant ratios to capitalization, and various ratios of operating expenses and revenues to each other and to plant investment.

FUNDS FOR RENEWALS AND REPLACEMENTS

In addition to O&M expenses, a utility must provide for capital costs on an annual basis. Capital costs represent the costs associated with investment in utility plant and includes a provision for ongoing renewals and replacements of the existing system.

Renewals and replacements typically include replacement of old service lines, small pumps, equipment, and minor capital expenditures that recur on an ongoing basis. The expenditure level should be developed carefully. Historic data may not necessarily represent a realistic level, particularly, if maintenance of system facilities has been deferred or neglected. Theoretically, an analysis between the level of maintenance expense associated with repairing existing plant and equipment versus annual capital cost associated with replacing old facilities should be conducted.

Renewal and Replacement Policy

Management should pursue a replacement policy that minimizes total costs and is consistent with rendering safe, reliable water service. Detailed cost and performance records will not always be available for evaluation. Consequently, awareness of the total cost-control objective by operating personnel and the financial manager is beneficial for planning purposes. The annual cost for normal renewals and replacements should be incorporated into budgets and cash-flow projections.

Provision for renewals and replacements of major facilities must also be incorporated into the financial planning process. Projects that constitute a significant commitment of financial resources will generally require funding from external sources. The effect on rates can be minimized if the utility investigates alternative funding options and analyzes the effects. Certain regulatory agencies will allow investor-owned utilities to include construction work in progress in the rate base, which eventually will result in lower total project costs and improved cash flow.

Comprehensive forecasts of revenues, expenses, and capital costs assist management with decisions regarding timing of rate increases and effects on customer bills. Furthermore, an effective planning process is fundamental to effective public relations with customers and regulatory agencies.

For investor-owned utilities with annual cash-flow deficiencies, special considerations are generally made in the rate-making process to allow for renewals and replacements. Over time, adequate funds available for renewals and replacements will benefit customers. For example, if service lines are replaced on a regular basis, water loss will be reduced. Conversely, if no attempt is made to identify leaks, service lines will only be replaced on an emergency basis. Unacceptable levels of water loss will occur through old deteriorated lines, resulting in wasted water, excessive pumping and chemical expense, and inefficient use of system capacity. Due to the long life of a water system plant and equipment, replacement of facilities can be delayed; however, delayed replacement can become an additional problem when costs for maintaining the worn out plant becomes excessive.

DEPRECIATION

Depreciation is the loss in value of property that is not restored by current maintenance. This loss in value is primarily due to wear and tear, decay, inadequacy, obsolescence, changes in demand for service, and requirements of public authorities.

Due to one or more of these factors, each element of the utility property must ultimately be retired and, if the utility is to remain whole, replaced.

Investor-owned utilities are permitted to include in revenue requirements an allowance, or provision, for annual depreciation. Depreciation allowances are established at levels that permit the systematic amortization of the original cost of the investment in various components of utility properties over their useful lives. Cash generated by recognition of depreciation charges is available for use to retire debt or to finance renewals and replacement expenditures. While such expenditures would preserve the overall original investment in properties, annual depreciation does not provide adequate capital to replace the investment in times of inflation. If annual depreciation allowances are not retained and reinvested, original investment may be gradually dissipated; and external financing requirements will be even greater than otherwise.

RETURN ON INVESTMENT

The total return on investment for an investor-owned utility must be sufficient to cover the cost of using various capital resources. These total costs of capital include interest and issuance cost of bonded indebtedness, dividends and issuance costs of preferred stock, and the cost of common equity. The first two components are established contractually and are easily determined from records of any specific utility.

The cost of common stock capital is frequently a controversial subject, as viewed by the utility, the consumer, and the regulatory agency. Ideologically, the cost of common stock capital is equal to the return required by investors, on their market-valued commitments, to continue to commit their capital resources to the enterprise. Since investors have differing views and expectations about the return to be realized on their common stock investments, determining the market rate of return that will attract capital is difficult and subject to special studies that recognize market conditions experienced.

CONSTRUCTION WORK IN PROGRESS

An item of major concern to investor-owned utilities today is the methodology used by regulatory agencies to recognize the costs associated with construction work in progress (CWIP). It is customary for some regulatory agencies to exclude CWIP from the rate base on which utilities are permitted to earn a return until such property is placed in service. In such instances, interest during construction is considered a part of the cost of the property, is capitalized, and becomes a part of the rate base.

Due to the unpredictable and erratic rates of inflation and interest costs, investor-owned utilities have sought relief from the administrative burden of charging interest during construction, by requesting the inclusion of CWIP in their rate base. This would allow earnings at the overall allowed rate of return. Many regulatory agencies now include at least some CWIP in the rate base, and permit the utility to earn a return thereon. When offset by other time-lag considerations, better matching of revenue requirements with revenues and invested funds occurs.

Chapter 7

Implementing a Financial Plan

Once management has chosen a financing alternative that best suits the utility's goals and objectives, the program must be implemented. Generally, if the plan involves rate revision and needs prior approval for debt issuance, the first step in the implementation process is to obtain approval of the appropriate governmental regulatory body. Regulatory bodies include local governments or state regulatory agencies. Successful approval of the financial plan also requires public support and input. Once an original or modified plan is approved, credit-agency review will also be required, if debt issues are to be rated.

LOCAL GOVERNMENT APPROVAL

Public officials who regulate utility planning and rates are normally elected representatives. In most cases, elected officials believe that their first responsibility is to their constituents and, secondarily, to the community as a whole. For this reason, the most successful way to sell capital-requirement needs and financial planning to local government is to first sell it to the general public.

Presenting Plans to the General Public

There are a number of avenues that the utility may take to present its plans to the general public. These include use of the news media—newspaper advertisements, press releases, and interviews; inserts in monthly utility bills; and neighborhood-level public presentations paralleling public officials' voting districts. No single method will reach all customers, thus, a combination of two or all three methods must be used.

Every water utility depends on public cooperation to achieve goals, which can only come about through clear communication. The utility's capital-requirement needs and financial plan should be carefully explained. The broad goals of presenting plans to the community include increased public awareness regarding the nature of the water system and the complex problems involved in meeting customer demands; appreciation of supplemental services provided, such as recreation or education; recognition of the necessity for wise use of a limited resource; understanding economic costs and other consequences of new projects; and other special areas of concern, as necessary.

If a water utility is to continue to provide a needed service and a quality product that is fairly priced and in a quantity and consistency that allows customers to maintain their current lifestyles, the utility must convince the customers that the utility serves them and not its own interests. Although utility management may believe that the utility has provided quality service for all citizens, the same perception may not be held by utility customers themselves.

All water utilities must create an environment that recognizes customers' needs and have the ability to identify and meet those needs. Management must translate the utility's needs into responses and results that meet the customers' needs if the utility is to win customer support. Customers should be provided with information that addresses all their concerns. In addition, utility management should carefully listen to what customers say and, where practical, incorporate concerns into the utility's strategic planning.

Presenting Plans to Public Officials

Once the utility customers have been presented with the utility's financial plan, the utility's plan and needs assessment must be presented to policymakers. Elected officials want to know that the public has been informed of the utility's plans and that they have had time to respond with their concerns. Public officials use the feedback received from their constituents, regarding the nature and amount of public opposition to utility planning, to formulate their decisions regarding the matter.

Utility management must show that they have a viable plan, have reviewed a number of capital and financing alternatives, and have selected the best plan to meet customer needs. It should be shown that, where practical, customer responses based on feedback have been incorporated into the financial plan. As part of its presentation, utility management must demonstrate that the utility is continually finding ways to keep costs low. In addition, the information presented to public officials should show the consequences of the utility doing nothing compared to implementing the financial plan.

Presentations to public officials should also provide an opportunity for the general public to state their concerns to the policymakers. Where disagreements exist between utility management and the general public, utility management should provide a strong argument for its proposed financing plan. Elected officials are then responsible to either support the plan before the public or provide policy direction on plan modifications.

REGULATORY AGENCY APPROVAL

Regulated investor-owned and publicly owned utilities both have the same need to present their financial plan to the public before presenting it to the regulatory agencies, which are comprised of elected or appointed officials who are generally consumer-oriented. Incorporating public concerns into capital requirements and financial planning will benefit the utility when rate relief is sought from the regulatory agency.

Utilities that are under the supervision of regulatory agencies use the same methods as local government-regulated utilities to inform and educate the public regarding the utility's needs and goals. The utility should demonstrate, through programs to enhance service, that the customers' welfare comes first. The capital program should show that oversizing is kept to a minimum, that the utility is expanding in stages to meet growth requirements, and that designs are energy-efficient system-wide. Ongoing efforts in O&M cost reductions should also be stressed.

Each presentation to regulatory agencies should be carefully planned and reviewed. Although regulatory agencies have specific presentation formats, the utility would be wise to prepare a parallel plan on a cash-needs basis. Such planning should realistically show all needs necessary to keep the utility in good financial condition. Requests for utility needs should be backed with historical experience, engineering reports, other appropriate material, and expert testimony.

National associations of investor-owned utilities and regulatory agencies maintain various ratio analyses, which are based on balance sheets and income statements from regulated utilities. This information is used to evaluate requests for rate relief according to industry standards. However, this information only indicates approximate rate levels permitted by regulatory-agency decisions. Such levels may not necessarily show that utility needs have been met. If regulated utilities share information on a cash-needs basis, then computed rates of return and capital structure ratios would be more meaningful.

RATING AGENCY APPROVAL

During periodic credit reviews and bond issuances, presentations to rating agencies, such as Moody's, S&P, and others, may be warranted in an attempt to upgrade the utility's credit rating or, at a minimum, maintain the present rating. A rating agency seeks assurances that, within the local environment in which the utility operates, management and local officials, or regulatory agencies, have adequately addressed the financial needs of the utility.

The agency is already aware of most local government problems through previous statistical reviews, making it necessary for the presenters to humanize their presentation. The utility should demonstrate that it is aware of the local problems it faces, has developed plausible answers and solutions to the problems, is in concert with local officials, and has a plan for addressing community-wide problems to the protection of bondholders and stockholders.

In order to obtain rating-agency approval, local government must demonstrate, on behalf of the utility, that it has been responsive to perceived needs of the community and has historically demonstrated a willingness to generate the required revenue to pay for the services rendered. At the same time, utility management should demonstrate that the projected capital requirements are designed to address community problems and meet customers' demand for service. Management should indicate where the financial plan addresses customer concerns, yet provides for sound financing of utility operations to the protection of bondholders and stockholders. Local officials, utility management, and outside financial and engineering consultants should be present to address specific questions posed by rating-agency analysts; a favorable impression will be made if the presenters anticipate analysts' questions.

PLANNING FOR CHANGE

One argument presented against detailed financial planning is that immediately on completion the plan is obsolete. The point to be recognized here is that situations change, so planning for change should be incorporated in a financial plan. Financial plans should be reviewed frequently, at least once each year and preferably before the annual budget process begins. The annual budget should reflect the implementation of the first year of the financing plan.

One way to cope with unforeseen changes is to maintain specific cash reserves for system emergencies or contingencies. Such reserves usually allow a utility to meet the contingency and still maintain a planned course of action. Another way to plan for change in the utility's capital requirements is to prioritize projects. If an unforeseen contingency arises, funds may be provided for it by deferring lower priority items. In this way, the impact on utility financing may be readily determined.

Contingency plans should be developed for hypothetical situations, and sensitivity analyses should be performed on the capital requirements and financial planning to determine the nature of impacts on the utility and the customers. Such exercises allow the utility to respond more quickly and more effectively to real emergencies.

Keeping up with current events will assist utility management in planning for change. Utility management must be aware of long-range plans and short-range actions of local government planning and zoning groups. The utility should have a good public relations program so that customer feedback may be incorporated into the utility's planning strategies. Finally, utility management should be active in national associations addressing utility matters. In this way, management can learn from the experiences of other utilities.

Many of the major changes currently facing utility operations are due to causes beyond the control of water utility management. Only by understanding that change is inevitable will utility management prepare to meet the challenge of change.

Glossary

accelerated depreciation Depreciation methods that amortize the cost of an asset at a faster rate than under the straight-line method. The three principal methods of accelerated depreciation are sum of the year's digits, double declining balance, and units of production.

accrual basis The basis of accounting under which revenues are recorded when earned and expenditures are recorded when they become liabilities for benefits received, notwithstanding that receipt of the revenue or payments of the expenditure may take place, in whole or in part, in another accounting period.

additional bonds test A statement in the bond indenture that stipulates requirements to be met before additional bonds can be issued with a parity claim on revenues already pledged.

ad valorem tax A state or local tax based on the assessed value of real or personal property.

advance for construction Advance made by or on behalf of customers or others for the purpose of construction, which are to be refunded either wholly or in part. When an applicant is refunded the entire amount to which he/she is entitled according to the agreement or rule under which the advance was made, the balance, if any, remaining in this account shall be credited to contribution in aid of construction.

advance refunding bonds Bonds issued to replace an outstanding bond issue prior to the date on which the outstanding bond becomes due or callable. Proceeds of the advance refunding bonds are deposited in escrow with a fiduciary, invested in US treasury bonds or other authorized securities, and used to redeem the underlying bonds at maturity or the call date and to pay interest on the bonds being refunded or the advance refunding bonds.

arbitrage bonds Any bond issue where any portion of the proceeds are reasonably expected (at the time of issuance) to be used directly or indirectly to acquire higher yielding investments or to replace funds that were used directly or indirectly to acquire higher-yielding investments (per IRS code, sec. 148).

authority bonds Bonds payable from the revenues of a specific authority. Since authorities usually have no revenues other than charges for services, their bonds are ordinarily revenue bonds.

betterment An addition made to or change made in a fixed asset that is expected to prolong its life or to increase its efficiency over and above that arising from maintenance. The cost of the betterment is added to the book value of the asset.

bond A written promise to pay a specified sum of money, called the face value or principal amount, at a specified date or dates in the future, called the maturity date(s), together with periodic interest at a specified rate. The difference between a note and a bond is that the latter runs for a longer period of time and requires greater legal formality.

bond anticipation notes Short-term interest-bearing notes issued by a governmental agency in anticipation of bonds to be issued at a later date. The notes are retired from proceeds of the bond issue to which they are related. *See* interim borrowing.

bond discount The excess of the face value of a bond above the price for which it is acquired or sold. The price does not include accrued interest at the date of acquisition or sale.

bond indenture/resolution/ordinance The legal instrument adopted by the issuer that concerns a bond issue. Typically, such instruments contain pledges to bondholders regarding the circumstances of payment of principal and interest, operation, flow of funds, and further debt issuance.

bond premium The excess of the price at which a bond is acquired or sold over its face value. The price does not include accrued interest at the date of acquisition or sale.

bonded debt That portion of indebtedness represented by outstanding bonds. *See* net bonded debt.

bonds payable The face value of bonds issued and unpaid.

budget An estimate of proposed expenditures for a given period or purpose and a statement of the means of financing them.

call The process of redeeming a bond or preferred stock issue before its normal maturity. Also, an option to buy (or call) a share of stock at a specified price within a specified period.

callable bond A bond that permits the issuer to pay the obligation before the stated maturity date by giving notice of redemption in a manner specified in the bond contract. Synonymous with *optional bond.*

call premium The amount of excess or par value that a company must pay when it calls a security.

capital grants Grants that are restricted by the grantor for the acquisition and/or construction of fixed assets.

capital outlays/expenditures Expenditures that result in the acquisition of or addition to fixed assets.

capital program A plan for capital expenditures to be incurred each year over a fixed period of years to meet capital needs arising from the long-term work program or otherwise. It sets forth each project or other contemplated expenditure in which the entity is to have a part and specifies the full resources estimated to be available to finance the projected expenditures.

cash basis The basis of accounting under which revenues are recorded when cash is received and expenditures are recorded when cash is disbursed.

certificates of participation A lease–purchase arrangement whereby the lessor issues certificates to third parties to finance property purchases, receives payment and retires debt in accordance with lease provisions, and incurs ownership liabilities. The local government lessee exercises control over the certificate features, makes payments for leased property, and may acquire the property through purchase options.

combination bond A bond issued by a government that is payable from the revenues of a governmental enterprise, but it is also backed by the full faith and credit of the government.

connection charge The charge made by the utility to recover the cost of connecting the customer's service line to the utility's facilities. This charge is often considered as contribution of capital by the customer or other agency applying for service; although it is most often considered as a utility revenue source. Refer to *system development charge* for the definition of another front-end fee sometimes levied on new applicants for service and called a connection charge.

construction work in progress (CWIP) The utility's investment in facilities under construction, but not yet dedicated to service. The inclusion of CWIP in rate base varies from one regulatory agency to another.

contribution in aid of construction Any amount of money, services, or property received by a water utility from any person or governmental agency that is provided at no cost to the utility. It represents an addition or transfer to the capital of the utility, and is used to offset the acquisition, improvement, or construction costs of the utility's property, facilities, or equipment used to provide utility services to the public. It includes amounts transferred from advances for construction representing any unrefunded balances of expired refund contracts or discounts resulting from termination of refund contracts. Contributions received from governmental agencies and others for relocation of water mains or other plant facilities are also included. All contributions are carried as equity capital in audited balance sheets of publicly owned utilities.

coupon bonds/bearer bonds A security that has no identification as to owner. It is presumed to be owned by the bearer of the bond. Such bonds are no longer issued since Congress required full registration of all new issues, effective July 1, 1983. Notes are still bearer-designated.

coupon rate The interest rate specified on interest coupons attached to a bond. The term is synonymous with *nominal interest rate*.

coverage ratios The margin of safety ratios, associated with bonded indebtedness and preferred stocks, reflecting the ratio of the actual or projected net revenue available for debt service to debt service or other costs. These ratios range from debt-service coverage of principal and interest, to interest only, to all fixed charges, including preferred stock dividends and lease payments. Coverage may be expressed as a ratio or as a percentage.

customer classification The grouping of customers into homogeneous classes. Typically, water utility customers may be classified as residential, commercial, and industrial for rate making and other purposes. For specific utilities, there may be a breakdown of these general classes into more specific groups. For example, the industrial class may be subdivided into small industry, large industry, and special. Some water systems have individual customers (large users) with individual water-use characteristics, service requirements, or other requirements that set them apart from other general customer classes and who may require a separate class designation. This may include large hospitals, universities, military establishments, and other such categories.

customer costs Customer costs vary with the number of customers served. These costs may include investment charges and expenses relative to a portion of the general distribution system, service-connection facilities, metering equipment, meter reading, billing, and accounting.

debenture A long-term debt instrument that is not secured by a mortgage on specific property.

debt An obligation resulting from the borrowing of money or from the purchase of goods and services.

debt burden Total debt as a fraction of total assessed valuation.

debt limit The maximum amount of gross or net debt that is legally permitted.

debt-service requirement The amount of money required to pay interest on outstanding debt, serial maturities of principal for serial bonds, and required contributions to accumulate monies for future retirement of term bonds.

debt-service reserve fund An account set up as a backup security for an issuer's bonds. This fund is used if revenues are insufficient to meet debt-service needs.

deep-discount bonds A discount is the amount by which the purchase price of a security is less than the principal amount or par value. Deep-discount bonds typically do not pay any annual interest; instead, the bondholder is rewarded in appreciation of the principal payable. *See* zero coupon/capital appreciation bonds.

default The failure to fulfill a contract. Generally, default refers to the failure to pay interest or principal on debt obligations.

deferred serial bonds Serial bonds in which the first installment does not fall due for two or more years from the date of issue.

depreciation The loss in service value not restored by current maintenance as applied to depreciable plant facilities. Depreciation is incurred in connection with the consumption or prospective retirement of plant facilities in the course of providing service. This depreciation is the result of causes known to be in current operation and against which the utility is not protected by insurance. Among the causes are wear and tear, decay, action of the elements, inadequacy, obsolescence, changes in the art, changes in demand, and requirements of public authorities. The proper level of depreciation expense at any given time should be based on the costs of depreciable plant in service. The funds resulting from depreciation are available for replacements, improvements, expansion of the system, or for repayment of the principal portion of outstanding debt.

direct debt The debt an entity has incurred in its own name or assumed through the annexation of territory or consolidation with another entity.

discount As applied to the securities issued or assumed by the utility, the excess of the par (stated value of no-par stocks) or face value of the securities plus interest or dividends accrued at the date of the sale over the cash value of the consideration received from their sale.

discount rate The interest rate used in the discounting process, also called capitalization rate.

earned surplus That part of surplus that has arisen out of accumulated net income, also called retained earnings.

effective interest rate The rate of earnings on a bond investment based on the actual price paid for the bond, the coupon rate, the maturity date, and the length of time between interest dates, in contrast with the nominal interest rate.

equity The net worth of a business, consisting of capital stock, capital (or paid in) surplus, earned surplus (or retained earnings), and, occasionally, certain net-worth reserves.

expenditures Amounts paid or incurred for all purposes, including expenses, provision for retirement of debt, and capital outlays.

financial advisor A consultant to an issuer of municipal securities who provides the issuer with advice on structure, timing, terms, and other similar matters concerning a new issue of securities.

full faith and credit A pledge of the general taxing power for the payment of debt obligations. Bonds carrying such pledges are referred to as general-obligation bonds or full-faith and credit bonds.

funding bonds Bonds issued to retire outstanding floating debt and to eliminate deficits.

general-obligation bonds Bonds for the payment of which the full faith and credit of the issuing government are pledged, implying (limited or unlimited) taxing powers to pay bondholders, if necessary.

improvements Buildings, other structures, and other attachments or annexations to land that are intended to remain so attached or annexed, such as sidewalks, trees, drives, tunnels, drains, and sewers.

industrial-aid bonds Bonds issued by governmental units, the proceeds of which are to construct plant facilities for private industrial concerns. Lease payments made by the industrial concern to the governmental unit are used to service the bonds.

interim borrowing Short-term loans to be repaid in the course of a fiscal year.

investor-owned water utility A utility owned by an individual, partnership, corporation, or other qualified entity with the equity provided by shareholders. Regulation may take the form of local or state jurisdiction.

lease–purchase agreements Contractual agreements that are termed "leases," but which in substance amount to purchase contracts.

letter of credit An irrevocable backup guarantee from a commercial bank on an issuer's credit in the form of a promise to stand behind the issuer's outstanding obligation if the issuer fails to provide sufficient funds for debt service.

long-term debt Debt with a maturity of more than one year after the date of issuance.

maintenance The upkeep necessary for efficient operation of physical properties. It involves labor and materials, but is not to be confused with betterment, replacement, or retirement.

marketable securities A highly liquid-type investment that can be sold at any time without interfering with normal operations of the business. Usually classified as a current asset, second only to cash in liquidity.

mortgage bonds Bonds secured by a mortgage against specified properties of an equity, usually its public utilities or other enterprises. If primarily payable from enterprise revenues, they are also classed as revenue bonds. *See* revenue bonds.

negotiated sale A bond issuance where the underwriters are chosen on a basis other than strictly price (as opposed to a competitive sale) and without an open bidding process. A negotiated underwriting involves extensive cooperation between underwriter and issuer. Sometimes called private placement.

net bonded debt Gross bonded debt less any cash or other assets available and earmarked for its retirement.

net income The excess of operating and nonoperating revenues over total of operating and nonoperating expenses for an accounting period. Synonomous with *retained earnings.*

net revenues available for debt service Operating revenues less O&M expenses but exclusive of depreciation and bond interest. Net revenue available for debt service as thus defined is used to compute coverage for revenue-bond issues. Under the laws of some states and the provisions of some revenue-bond indentures, net revenues available for debt service for computation of revenue-bond coverage must be computed on a cash basis rather than in conformity with generally accepted accounting principles (GAAP). Sometimes, indenture provisions permit the inclusion of nonoperating revenue and system-development-charge receipts with operating revenue when determining net revenue available for debt service. *See* coverage.

nominal interest rate The contractual interest rate shown on the face and in the body of a bond and representing the amount of interest to be paid, in contrast to the effective interest rate. *See* coupon rate.

nonoperating expenses Expenses incurred in the performance of activities not directly related to supplying the basic service by an enterprise. Also referred to as other expenses or other deductions on financial statements.

nonoperating revenue Income of the utility that is not derived from normal operations, such as rents from nonutility facilities, interest on investments or on bank time deposits, and revenue for rendering nonutility services to others. This is also referred to as other income in financial statements.

note payable In general, an unconditional written promise signed by the maker to pay a certain sum in money on demand or at a fixed or determinable time either to the bearer or to the order of a person designated therein. *See* temporary loans.

obsolescence The decrease in the value of fixed assets resulting from economic, social, technological, or legal changes.

operating expenses Generally, the total of operation expense, maintenance expense, annual depreciation, amortization expense, income taxes, and taxes other than income taxes.

operating revenues Revenues derived directly from the operations of the utility, either from the sale of water or closely allied activities.

operation expense Costs incurred in operating source-of-supply facilities, pumping facilities, water purification facilities, and transmission and distribution facilities plus costs for customer accounting, customer services, administration, and general.

ordinance A formal legislative enactment by the council or governing body of a municipality. It has the full force and effect of law within the boundaries of the municipality to which it applies.

pass-through bonds Bonds issued by an agency acting as an issuing party, but which does not assume any obligation on debt repayment.

paying agent Place where the principal and interest are payable, usually a bank designated by the issuer or the office of the issuer's treasurer.

perpetual inventory A system whereby the inventory of units of property at any date may be obtained directly from the records without resorting to an actual physical count.

premium As applied to the securities issued or assumed by the utility, the excess of the cash value of the consideration received from their sale over the sum of their par (stated value of nonpar stocks) or face value and interest or dividends accrued at the date of sale.

publicly owned water utility A water utility created by the state or other governmental legislative action, with the mandate that the purposes of the utility are public purposes and that its functions are essential governmental proprietary functions. Its primary purpose is to provide its designated area with potable water in an adequate supply at reasonable costs so that people of the area may improve their health, safety, and welfare. A publicly owned water utility may be part of a municipal government operation, a county agency, a regional authority, or take such other forms as is appropriate for its service area.

rate base The value of a water utility's property used in computing an authorized return under the applicable laws and/or regulatory policies of the agency setting rates for the utility.

rate covenants A legal commitment by a bond issuer to maintain rates at certain levels, which is necessary to generate a specified level of revenue or a ratio of revenue to debt service, or interest. Rate covenants can be designated on a ratio of gross revenues or net revenue to debt-service basis.

rating agencies Independent agencies engaged by issuers to offer credit information and analysis on a particular bond or note issue. The two largest are Moody's Investors Service, Inc., and the Standard & Poor's Corporation.

ratings Designations used by investor services to give relative indications of credit quality, ranging from highest (Aaa/AAA) to noninvestment grade (Ba/BB+ or below).

refunding bonds Bonds issued to retire bonds already outstanding. The refunding bonds may be sold for cash and outstanding bonds redeemed in cash, or the refunding bonds may be exchanged with holders of outstanding bonds.

registered bonds A bond whose owner or holder is recorded with the issuer or the trustee of the issuer so that payment of principal or interest or both may be made only to the registered holder. All new tax-exempt bonds are fully registered since July 1, 1983. Transfer of ownership is a more complicated process with registered bonds relative to coupon or bearer bonds.

retirement unit Those items of utility property that, when retired with or without replacement, are accounted for by crediting the book costs to the appropriate utility plant account. In general, any item of property that is readily separable, and separately useful, from a larger assembly of which it forms a part should be treated as a retirement unit. The cost of replacing property components smaller than a retirement unit becomes a maintenance expense.

revenue bonds A bond payable solely from net or gross nontax revenues derived from tolls, charges, or rents paid by users of the facility constructed with the proceeds of the bond issue.

serial annuity bonds Serial bonds in which the annual installments of bond principal are so arranged that the combined payments for principal and interest are approximately the same each year.

serial bonds Bonds whose principal is repaid in periodic installments over the life of the issue.

service life The time between the date utility plant is includable in utility plant in service or utility plant leased to others and the date of its retirement. If depreciation is accounted for on a production basis rather than on a time basis, service life should be measured in terms of the appropriate unit of production.

sinking fund bonds Bonds issued under an agreement that requires the entity to set aside, periodically out of its revenues, a sum that, with compound earnings thereon, will be sufficient to redeem the bonds at their stated date of maturity. Sinking fund bonds are usually term bonds.

straight serial bonds Serial bonds in which the annual installments of bond principal are about equal.

surety bond A written promise to pay damages or to indemnify against losses caused by the party or parties named in the document, through nonperformance or through defalcation.

surplus The amount by which the assets of a private utility exceed the total of its liabilities, reserves, and capital stock. In a publicly owned utility, the amount by which the assets exceed the total liabilities, reserves, and municipal equity.

system-development charge A contribution of capital towards recently completed or planned future backup plant facilities necessary to meet the service needs of new customers to which such fees apply. Two methods used to determine the amount of these charges are the buy-in method and incremental-cost pricing method. Various terms have been used to describe these charges in the industry, but regardless of the term used, these charges have the purpose of providing funds to be used to finance all or part of capital improvements necessary to serve new customers and are raised outside of capital to be served from general water-use rates.

tax-exempt commercial paper A short-term promissory note, usually not exceeding 270 days, that may be rolled over to new maturities and must be backed by a credit facility. Commercial paper is issued for working capital purposes or for bridging periods before bond issuance.

temporary loans Short-term obligations representing amounts borrowed for short periods of time and usually evidenced by notes payable or warrants payable. They may be unsecured or secured by specific revenues to be collected.

tender-option bond (put bond) A bond that can be redeemed by the bondholder on a date or dates prior to the stated maturity date. Also known as a demand bond.

term bonds Bonds with entire principal maturing on one date.

trustee A bank designated by the issuer as the custodian of funds and official representative of the bondholders. Trustees uphold the interest of the bondholders in matters of compliance with the terms of the contract between issuer and bondholders.

underwriters The single purchaser or group of purchasers of a note or bond who hold the issue for reselling to the general public.

variable-rate demand bonds An issue whose payable interest rate is allowed to rise or fall with market conditions. In addition, these bonds have "put" provisions, allowing the investor to redeem them at any time.

warrant An order drawn by the legislative body or an officer of a governmental unit on its treasurer directing the latter to pay a specified amount to the person named or to the bearer. This would apply to holders of bonds with warrants attached.

working capital Cash, materials, supplies, and other similar current assets necessary in the operation of the enterprise. It is usually measured by the excess of current assets over the current liabilities or sometimes as a portion of annual O&M expense levels.

work order A written order authorizing and directing the performance of a certain task and issued to the person who is to direct the work. Items of information shown on the order are the nature and location of the job, specifications of the work to be performed, and the work order number that is referred to in reporting the amount of labor, materials, and equipment used.

yield The rate of return on an investment; the internal rate of return; dividends paid out during a year divided by the number of outstanding shares of common stock at the year end; interest or other return from an investment. *See* effective interest rate.

yield curve The graphic depiction of the series of annual returns to investors.

zero-coupon/capital-appreciation bonds A bond in which no current or annual interest is paid; the bondholder receives an amount at maturity that reflects compounded interest at a specified rate. *See* deep-discount bond.

Index